Usb

# First Illustrated English Dictionary

Rachel Ward and Jane Bingham

Illustrated by Villie Karabatzia

Designed by Karen Tomlins

Edited by Phil Clarke, Sam Smith and Sam Taplin

Advisors: John McIlwain, Rita D'Apice Gould and Porter Tierney

# USING YOUR DICTIONARY

## Finding a word

The words in this dictionary are arranged in alphabetical order from A to Z. This helps you to find them easily.

**1** To find a word, such as "beach", think of its first letter, "b".

**2** Now look at the alphabet bar down the side of each page. When you see a coloured letter "b" you have found the pages of "b" words.

**3** Next, think of the second letter of your word. Look along the top of the page for words that begin "be".

**4** Then look down the "be" words until you find your word.

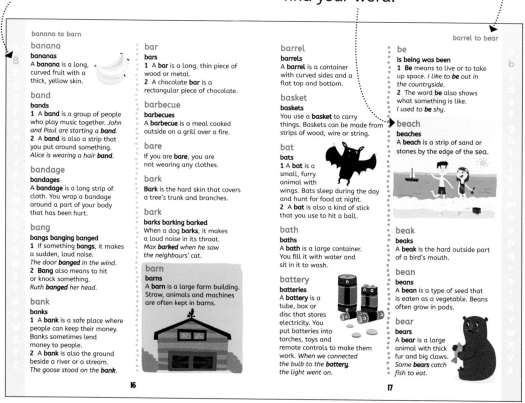

banana to barn

**banana**
**bananas**
A **banana** is a long, curved fruit with a thick, yellow skin.

**band**
**bands**
1 A **band** is a group of people who play music together. *John and Paul are starting a band.*
2 A **band** is also a strip that you put around something. *Alice is wearing a hair band.*

**bandage**
**bandages**
A **bandage** is a long strip of cloth. You wrap a bandage around a part of your body that has been hurt.

**bang**
**bangs banging banged**
1 If something **bangs**, it makes a sudden, loud noise. *The door banged in the wind.*
2 Bang also means to hit or knock something. *Ruth banged her head.*

**bank**
**banks**
1 A **bank** is a safe place where people can keep their money. Banks sometimes lend money to people.
2 A **bank** is also the ground beside a river or a stream. *The goose stood on the bank.*

**bar**
**bars**
1 A **bar** is a long, thin piece of wood or metal.
2 A chocolate **bar** is a rectangular piece of chocolate.

**barbecue**
**barbecues**
A **barbecue** is a meal cooked outside on a grill over a fire.

**bare**
If you are **bare**, you are not wearing any clothes.

**bark**
**Bark** is the hard skin that covers a tree's trunk and branches.

**bark**
**barks barking barked**
When a dog **barks**, it makes a loud noise in its throat. *Max barked when he saw the neighbours' cat.*

**barn**
**barns**
A **barn** is a large farm building. Straw, animals and machines are often kept in barns.

**barrel**
**barrels**
A **barrel** is a container with curved sides and a flat top and bottom.

**basket**
**baskets**
You use a **basket** to carry things. Baskets can be made from strips of wood, wire or string.

**bat**
**bats**
1 A **bat** is a small, furry animal with wings. Bats sleep during the day and hunt for food at night.
2 A **bat** is also a kind of stick that you use to hit a ball.

**bath**
**baths**
A **bath** is a large container. You fill it with water and sit in it to wash.

**battery**
**batteries**
A **battery** is a tube, box or disc that stores electricity. You put batteries into torches, toys and remote controls to make them work. *When we connected the bulb to the battery, the light went on.*

**be**
**is being was been**
1 **Be** means to live or to take up space. *I like to be out in the countryside.*
2 The word **be** also shows what something is like. *I used to be shy.*

**beach**
**beaches**
A **beach** is a strip of sand or stones by the edge of the sea.

**beak**
**beaks**
A **beak** is the hard outside part of a bird's mouth.

**bean**
**beans**
A **bean** is a type of seed that is eaten as a vegetable. Beans often grow in pods.

**bear**
**bears**
A **bear** is a large animal with thick fur and big claws. *Some bears catch fish to eat.*

barrel to bear

16

17

---

If you can't find a word, you may have spelt it wrongly. For example:

- **Ceiling** and **city** begin with an "**s**" sound, but are spelt "**ce**" and "**ci**".
- **Knee** and **knife** begin with an "**n**" sound but are spelt "**kn**".
- **Phone** and **photograph** begin with an "**f**" sound, but are spelt "**ph**".

## Looking at a word

The dictionary tells you lots of things about words and how to use them.

- You can check how to spell a word.

**new**

**newer newest**

**1** If something is **new**, it has just been made or it has just been bought. *Ruby has a **new** bicycle.*

**2** **New** can also mean different. *There is a **new** family next door.*

■ *opposite* **old**

- You can see other ways of using the word.
- You can find out what the word means.
- You can see how the word is used.
- You can find out if a word has more than one meaning.
- You can see the opposites of some words.

## More help with words

Here are some more ways that this dictionary helps you with writing and saying words.

- It gives you ideas for other words to use in your writing.

  Some other words for **big** are **enormous**, **gigantic**, **huge**, **massive** and **vast**.

- It helps you say difficult words.

**yolk**

**yolks**
▲ *say yoke*
The **yolk** is the yellow part in the middle of an egg.

## Alphabetical order

It's much easier to use a dictionary if you know how to put words into alphabetical order. You compare their first letters, then their second letters, then their third, and so on.

For example, the words bed, ant, bedtime, bear, bad and bedroom are put into alphabetical order like this:

| | |
|---|---|
| **ant** | a comes before b |
| **bad** | ba comes before be |
| **bear** | bea comes before bed |
| **bed** | bed comes before bedr |
| **bedroom** | bedr comes before bedt |
| **bedtime** | |

# Aa

## able

If you are **able** to do something, you know how to do it. *Zak is able to ride a bicycle.*

## about

1 **About** means to do with something. *This book is about elephants.*
2 **About** also means near to something. *The party ends at about six o'clock.*

## above

If something is **above** another thing, it is over it or higher than it. *The balloons are above the clouds.*
■ opposite **below**

## abroad

When you go **abroad**, you go to another country.

## absent

If someone is **absent**, they are not here. *Joe is absent from school today because he is sick.*

## accident

accidents
1 If there is an **accident**, something bad happens that you do not expect. *Rosa had an accident and broke her leg.*
2 If something happens **by accident**, nobody has planned or expected it. *I met my friend Peter by accident.*

## ache

aches aching ached
▲ *rhymes with* **cake**
If part of your body **aches**, it hurts for a while. *Skating makes my legs ache.*

## across

**Across** means from one side to the other. *Owen walked across the road.*

## act

acts acting acted
1 When you **act**, you do something. *Ranjit acted quickly to put out the fire.*
2 If you **act** in a play, you pretend to be one of the people in it.

## action

actions
1 An **action** is a movement. *We all copied Simon's actions.*
2 An **action** is anything that is done. *My dad was given a medal for his brave actions.*

## activity

**activities**
An **activity** is something that you do. *Horse riding is my favourite activity.*

## add

**adds adding added**
**1** If you **add** something to another thing, you put it with that thing. ***Add** butter to the flour.*
**2** When you **add** numbers, you put them together. *Jane **added** five and seven to make twelve.*

$$5+7=12$$

■ *opposite* **subtract**

## address

**addresses**
Your **address** is the name of the place where you live.

Father Christmas
Santa's Grotto
Reindeerland
XM4 5HQ

## admire

**admires admiring admired**
If you **admire** someone or something, you think that they are very nice or very good. *Jake **admired** Rachel's painting.*

## admit

**admits admitting admitted**
When you **admit** that you did something, you agree that you did it.

## adopt

**adopts adopting adopted**
When people **adopt** a child, the child comes to live with them and becomes part of their family.

## adore

**adores adoring adored**
If you **adore** something, you love it very much. *Katie **adores** dogs.*

## adult

**adults**
An **adult** is a grown-up person.

adult

child

## adventure

**adventures**
An **adventure** is something exciting that people do. Some adventures can be dangerous. *Exploring the castle was a great **adventure**.*

## advice

**Advice** is information that is meant to help you. *My granny gave me some good **advice**.*

## aeroplane

**aeroplanes**
An **aeroplane** is a large machine that flies through the air. Aeroplanes have wings and engines. They carry people or things from one place to another.

**5**

a
b
c
d
e
f
g
h
i
j
k
l
m
n
o
p
q
r
s
t
u
v
w
x
y
z

**A**

## affect

**affects affecting affected**
If something **affects** another thing, it does something to it. *Feeling nervous affected June's singing.*

## afford

**affords affording afforded**
If you can **afford** something, you have enough money to buy it.

## afraid

If you're **afraid**, you're worried something might go wrong, or something might hurt you. *Jessie is afraid of spiders.*

## after

**1** When one thing happens **after** another, it happens later than it. *We went for a walk after lunch.*
■ *opposite* **before**
**2 After** also means following something. *William ran after the ball.*

## afternoon

**afternoons**
The **afternoon** is the part of the day that starts at 12 o'clock and ends at about 6 o'clock.

## again

If you do something **again**, you do it one more time. *Beth is singing that song again.*

## against

**1** If something is **against** another thing, it is next to it and touching it. *Benji leant his bike against the wall.*
**2** If you are **against** someone or something, you are on a different side from them. *The teams will play against each other tomorrow.*
**3** If you are playing a game and you do something **against the rules**, you do not obey the rules.

## age

**ages**
Your **age** is how old you are. *At the age of five, you have five candles on your birthday cake.*

## ago

**Ago** means before now. *We started school two weeks ago.*

## agree

**agrees agreeing agreed**
**1** If you **agree** with someone, you both think the same about something. *Garth and I agreed that the film was dreadful.*
■ *opposite* **disagree**
**2** If you **agree** to do something that someone has asked you to, you say that you will do it. *Jon agreed to tidy his room before he went out.*
■ *opposite* **refuse**

# ahead

If you are **ahead** of someone, you are in front of them. *Skye ran on **ahead** of the others. Grace is **ahead** of Daisy in maths.*

# aim

**aims aiming aimed**
When you **aim** something, you try to make it go in a particular direction. *Robin **aimed** the arrow and fired.*

# air

**Air** is what you breathe. You cannot see air but it is a mixture of gases all around you.

# aircraft

**aircraft**
An **aircraft** is a machine that flies.

# airport

**airports**
An **airport** is a place where aircraft take off and land.

# alarm

**alarms**
An **alarm** is something that makes a loud noise. Alarms wake you up or warn you about something.
*An **alarm** clock.
A fire **alarm**.*

# album

**albums**
An **album** is a collection of recorded songs.

# alien

**aliens**
In stories, an **alien** is a creature that comes from another planet. *The **alien** had three eyes and four arms.*

# alike

If people or things are **alike**, they are the same in some way. *The twins look **alike**.*

# alive

If a person, an animal, or a plant is **alive**, they are living.
■ *opposite* **dead**

# all

**All** means everything, everyone, or the whole thing. *All the children were excited. Karen ate all the chocolate.*

# alligator

**alligators**
An **alligator** is a large reptile that looks similar to a crocodile.

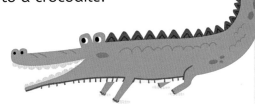

A
B
C
D
E
F
G
H
I
J
K
L
M
N
O
P
Q
R
S
T
U
V
W
X
Y
Z

## allow

**allows allowing allowed**
If someone **allows** you to do something, they let you do it. *Mum **allowed** us to stay up late.*

## almost

**Almost** means close to, but not quite. *It's **almost** bedtime.*

## alone

When you are **alone**, you are not with anyone else.

## along

1  **Along** means from one end to the other. *The cat ran **along** the street.*
2  If you bring something **along**, you bring it with you. *George brought his dog **along** to school.*

## aloud

When you read **aloud**, you read so that other people can hear you. *Ollie is reading his poem **aloud**.*

## alphabet

**alphabets**
An **alphabet** is a set of all the letters that people use to write words. You can see the order of the letters in the English alphabet at the side of this page.

## already

If something has happened **already**, it has happened before now. *I've seen this film **already**.*

## alright

1  Something that is **alright** is good enough. *Does this hat look **alright**?*
2  **Alright** also means well and happy. *Are you feeling **alright**?*

## also

You use the word **also** to mean something extra. *Hannah ate an apple. She **also** ate my banana.*

## always

If you **always** do something, you do it all the time or every time. *I **always** read before I go to sleep.*
■ opposite **never**

## amazing

Something that is **amazing** is very surprising or impressive. *Dan scored an **amazing** goal.*

## ambulance

**ambulances**
An **ambulance** is a special van that takes injured or sick people to hospital.

## amount

**amounts**
An **amount** is how much there is of something. *Sarah ate a tiny amount of ice cream.*

## anchor

**anchors**
▲ *say an-ker*
An **anchor** is a heavy, metal hook on a long chain that is fixed to a ship. When the anchor is thrown off a ship, it sinks to the bottom of the sea and stops the ship from moving.

## angry

**angrier angriest**
If you are **angry**, you are very annoyed and feel like shouting or fighting. *Kim was angry when she saw that her glasses were broken.*

## animal

**animals**
An **animal** is anything that moves and breathes. Horses, lizards, fish, birds and insects are all animals. Plants are not animals.

## ankle

**ankles**
Your **ankle** is the joint between your leg and your foot.

## annoy

**annoys annoying annoyed**
If someone or something **annoys** you, they make you feel angry. *Ed annoyed his brother by singing out of tune.*

## another

**1** You use the word **another** to mean one more. *Please may I have another biscuit?*
**2** You also use **another** to mean a different one. *Is there another way to the station?*

## answer

**answers**
An **answer** is what you say after someone has asked you a question. *Hari gave the right answer to the question.*

## ant

**ants**
An **ant** is a small insect. Ants live in large groups in the ground or in trees. *Some ants bite leaves off trees and carry them back to their nest.*

a
b
c
d
e
f
g
h
i
j
k
l
m
n
o
p
q
r
s
t
u
v
w
x
y
z

**A**
B
C
D
E
F
G
H
I
J
K
L
M
N
O
P
Q
R
S
T
U
V
W
X
Y
Z

## any

**1 Any** means some. *Are there any biscuits left?*
**2** You also use the word **any** to show that it does not matter which one. *Take any book you like.*

## anybody

**Anybody** means any person. *Has anybody seen my slippers?*

## anyone

**Anyone** means any person. *Anyone is welcome to come to the party.*

## anyway

If you do something **anyway**, you do it even though there are reasons not to. *Bella had no umbrella, but went out in the rain anyway.*

## anywhere

**Anywhere** means any place. *I can't find my slippers anywhere!*

## apart

**1 Apart** means away from something else. *Stand with your feet apart.*
**2** If you take something **apart**, you take it to pieces. *Ben is taking his bicycle apart to see how it works.*
**3 Apart from** means except. *Everyone enjoyed the film, apart from Milo.*

## ape

**apes**
An **ape** is a large animal with long arms and no tail. Chimpanzees and gorillas are apes.

## apologize

**apologizes apologizing apologized**
When you **apologize**, you say sorry for something that you have done or said. *Mark apologized for breaking the chair.*

## app

**apps**
An **app** is a program on a smartphone or tablet. App is short for application.

## appear

**appears appearing appeared**
When something **appears**, it can be seen when it could not be seen before.
■ *opposite*
**disappear**

*Two birds appeared from inside the hat.*

## apple

**apples**
An **apple** is a rounded fruit with a green, red or yellow skin.

## apron

**aprons**
You wear an **apron** to keep your clothes clean when you are cooking or painting.

## aquarium

**aquariums**
An **aquarium** is a glass tank filled with water. You keep fish and other creatures in an aquarium.

## area

**areas**
An **area** is a place or a space. *A large **area** of grass.*
*A science **area**.*

## aren't

**Aren't** is a short way of saying **are not**. *These strawberries **aren't** ripe yet.*

## argue

**argues arguing argued**
People **argue** because they do not agree about something. When they argue, they say what they think and often get angry. *We **argued** about which team was the best.*

## argument

**arguments**
An **argument** is when people don't agree with each other. When people have an argument, they say what they think and often get angry.

## arm

**arms**
Your **arm** is the part of your body between your shoulder and your hand.

## armchair

**armchairs**
An **armchair** is a comfortable chair with parts on either side for you to rest your arms on.

## armour

**Armour** is a set of clothes made of metal. Soldiers long ago wore armour to protect themselves when they were fighting.

**A**
B C D E F G H I J K L M N O P Q R S T U V W X Y Z

## army

**armies**

An **army** is a large group of people who fight on the same side in a war.

## around

1 **Around** something means in a circle all the way along its outside. *Mo tied a ribbon **around** her waist.*

2 **Around** also means in every part. *I looked **around** the house.*

3 **Around** also means near to somewhere. *Kai lives **around** here.*

## arrange

**arranges arranging arranged**

1 When you **arrange** something, you plan how it will be done. *Mum is **arranging** a party for next weekend.*

2 If you **arrange** things, you put them together so they look tidy or pretty.

*Rana arranged the flowers in a vase.*

## arrive

**arrives arriving arrived**

When something or someone **arrives**, they get to where they are going. *The parcel **arrived** at Lily's house. We **arrived** at the park.*

## arrow

**arrows**

1 An **arrow** is a thin stick with a point at one end and feathers at the other end. You shoot arrows from a bow.

2 An **arrow** is also a sign that shows you which way to go. *Follow the **arrows** to get to the sports hall.*

## art

**Art** is something that someone has made to be beautiful, or to show feelings or ideas. Paintings and statues are types of art.

## ask

**asks asking asked**

1 If you **ask** a question, you say that you want to know something. *Jack **asked** me how old I was.*

2 If you **ask for** something, you say that you want it. *Mia **asked for** an apple.*

## asleep

When you are **asleep**, your eyes are closed and your whole body is resting. *Pickle is **asleep** on a cushion.*

■ opposite
**awake**

## assembly

**assemblies**

An **assembly** is a large group of people who are meeting together. *School **assembly**.*

# astonish

**astonishes astonishing astonished**
If you **astonish** someone, you make them feel very surprised.

## astronaut

**astronauts**
An **astronaut** is someone who goes into space. Astronauts travel in spacecraft.

# ate

**Ate** comes from the word **eat**. *Usually we eat at home. Yesterday we **ate** at a restaurant.*

# atlas

**atlases**
An **atlas** is a book of maps.

# attach

**attaches attaching attached**
When you **attach** one thing to another, you join them together. *Will **attached** the lead to Fido's collar.*

# attack

**attacks attacking attacked**
If someone **attacks** another person, they try to hurt them.

# attention

**attention**
When you pay **attention**, you watch and listen carefully. *Pay **attention** to what I'm saying!*

# attic

attic

**attics**
An **attic** is a room at the top of a house, just under the roof.

# attract

**attracts attracting attracted**
When a magnet **attracts** an object, it makes it come nearer.

# audience

**audiences**
An **audience** is a group of people who watch or listen to something, such as a play or a band.

# aunt

**aunts**
Your **aunt** is the sister of your mum or your dad. Another word for aunt is auntie.

# autumn

▲ *say **aw**-tum*
**Autumn** is one of the four seasons. It comes between summer and winter. In autumn, the weather begins to get cold and leaves fall from the trees.

A
B
C
D
E
F
G
H
I
J
K
L
M
N
O
P
Q
R
S
T
U
V
W
X
Y
Z

## awake

**Awake** means not asleep. *Owls stay awake at night and sleep in the day.*
■ opposite **asleep**

## away

1 If someone or something goes **away**, they go from where they are to another place.
2 If you put things **away**, you put them where they belong. *Finlay, put your toys away.*

## awful

Something that is **awful** is very bad. *That programme was awful.*

## awkward

1 Something that is **awkward** is difficult to use. *My shoelaces are awkward to tie because they are too short.*
2 Someone who moves in an **awkward** way is clumsy.
3 Someone who behaves in an **awkward** way is very hard to please.

## axe

**axes**
An **axe** is a tool with a long handle and a large, metal blade. People use axes to chop wood.

## baby

**babies**
A **baby** is a very young child.

## baby-sitter

**baby-sitters**
A **baby-sitter** is someone who looks after children when their parents are out.

## back

**backs**
1 The **back** of something is the part farthest from the front. *We sat at the back of the cinema.*
2 Your **back** is the part of your body between your neck and your bottom.
■ opposite **front**

## backwards

1 If a word is spelt **backwards**, it is spelt the wrong way round. "Step" spelt backwards is "pets".
2 If you move **backwards**, you move the way that your back faces. *Jack is walking backwards through the snow.*
■ opposite **forwards**

# bacon

**Bacon** is a type of meat that comes from a pig.

# bad

**worse worst**
1 Someone who is **bad** does things that they should not do.
2 Something that is **bad** is not good. *A **bad** cold.*

■ opposite **good**

Some other words for **bad** are **awful**, **terrible**, and **dreadful**.

# badge

**badges**
A **badge** is a small piece of metal, plastic or cloth that you wear on your clothes.

# badger

**badgers**
A **badger** is a black and white animal that lives under the ground.

# bag

**bags**
You use a **bag** to hold or carry things. *A shopping **bag**.*

# bake

**bakes baking baked**
When you **bake** food, you cook it in an oven. *Maggie **baked** a cake.*

# balance

**balances balancing balanced**
If you **balance** something, you keep it steady so it does not fall. *The seal **balanced** a ball on its nose.*

# bald

**balder baldest**
People who are **bald** have little or no hair on the top of their heads.

# ball

**balls**
A **ball** is a round object that you throw, catch or kick.

tennis ball

# ballet

▲ *say **bal**-ay*
**Ballet** is a kind of dance with special steps. Ballet often tells a story.

# balloon

**balloons**
1 A **balloon** is a thin, rubber bag. When you blow into a balloon, it gets bigger.
2 A **balloon** is also a kind of aircraft powered by a very large bag of hot air. Passengers ride in a basket underneath it.

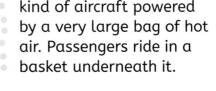

## banana

**bananas**

A **banana** is a long, curved fruit with a thick, yellow skin.

## band

**bands**

1 A **band** is a group of people who play music together. *John and Paul are starting a **band**.*
2 A **band** is also a strip that you put around something. *Alice is wearing a hair **band**.*

## bandage

**bandages**

A **bandage** is a long strip of cloth. You wrap a bandage around a part of your body that has been hurt.

## bang

**bangs banging banged**

1 If something **bangs**, it makes a sudden, loud noise. *The door **banged** in the wind.*
2 **Bang** also means to hit or knock something. *Ruth **banged** her head.*

## bank

**banks**

1 A **bank** is a safe place where people can keep their money. Banks sometimes lend money to people.
2 A **bank** is also the ground beside a river or a stream. *The goose stood on the **bank**.*

## bar

**bars**

1 A **bar** is a long, thin piece of wood or metal.
2 A chocolate **bar** is a rectangular piece of chocolate.

## barbecue

**barbecues**

A **barbecue** is a meal cooked outside on a grill over a fire.

## bare

If you are **bare**, you are not wearing any clothes.

## bark

**Bark** is the hard skin that covers a tree's trunk and branches.

## bark

**barks barking barked**

When a dog **barks**, it makes a loud noise in its throat. *Max **barked** when he saw the neighbours' cat.*

## barn

**barns**

A **barn** is a large farm building. Straw, animals and machines are often kept in barns.

## barrel
**barrels**
A **barrel** is a container with curved sides and a flat top and bottom.

## basket
**baskets**
You use a **basket** to carry things. Baskets can be made from strips of wood, wire or string.

## bat
**bats**

1 A **bat** is a small, furry animal with wings. Bats sleep during the day and hunt for food at night.
2 A **bat** is also a kind of stick that you use to hit a ball.

## bath
**baths**
A **bath** is a large container. You fill it with water and sit in it to wash.

## battery
**batteries**
A **battery** is a tube, box or disc that stores electricity. You put batteries into torches, toys and remote controls to make them work. *When we connected the bulb to the battery, the light went on.*

## be
**is being was been**
1 **Be** means to live or to take up space. *I like to be out in the countryside.*
2 The word **be** also shows what something is like. *I used to be shy.*

## beach
**beaches**
A **beach** is a strip of sand or stones by the edge of the sea.

## beak
**beaks**
A **beak** is the hard outside part of a bird's mouth.

## bean
**beans**
A **bean** is a type of seed that is eaten as a vegetable. Beans often grow in pods.

## bear
**bears**
A **bear** is a large animal with thick fur and big claws. *Some bears catch fish to eat.*

## beard

**beards**
A **beard** is the hair that grows on a man's chin and cheeks.

## beat

**beats beating beat beaten**
**1** If you **beat** someone in a race or a competition, you do better than they do.
**2** If you **beat** something, you keep hitting it.

*Stuart **beat** his drum.*

## beautiful

▲ *say **byoo**-tih-ful*
If something is **beautiful**, it is lovely to look at or listen to.

## beaver

**beavers**
A **beaver** is an animal with very sharp front teeth and a large, flat tail. Beavers build their homes in rivers out of sticks and mud.

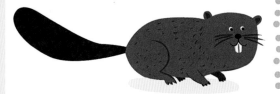

## became

**Became** comes from the word **become**. *I thought she might become famous, but she **became** a huge celebrity.*

## because

You use the word **because** to explain why something happens. *I was scared **because** it was dark.*

## become

**becomes becoming became become**
If one thing **becomes** something else, it turns into it. *Some caterpillars **become** butterflies.*

## bed

**beds**
A **bed** is something that you lie on when you sleep or rest.

## bedroom

**bedrooms**
Your **bedroom** is the room where you sleep.

## bee

**bees**
A **bee** is an insect with black and yellow stripes. Some bees make honey. Bees can sting, but rarely do.

## beef

**Beef** is meat that comes from a cow.

## beetle

**beetles**
A **beetle** is a common insect. There are thousands of different beetles.

## before

If something happens **before** something else, it happens earlier than it.
■ *opposite* **after**

## begin

**begins beginning began begun**
When you **begin** to do something, you start to do it. *Jo **began** to cry.*

## behave

**behaves behaving behaved**
1 The way you **behave** is the way that you do things. *Annie is **behaving** very strangely today.*
2 If you **behave yourself**, you do what you are supposed to.

## behind

1 If you are **behind** something, you are further back than it. *Mike was **behind** Sam in the race.*
2 **Behind** also means round the back of. *Ramel hid **behind** the shed.*

## believe

**believes believing believed**
If you **believe** something, you think that it is true. *Patrick **believed** Buster's story.*

## bell

**bells**
A **bell** is a metal object shaped like a cup. Bells make a ringing noise when you hit them or shake them.

## belong

**belongs belonging belonged**
1 If something **belongs** to you, it is yours. *This hat **belongs** to me.*
2 If you **belong** to a club, you are a member of it.
3 If something **belongs** in a place, that is where it should be. *The spade **belongs** in the shed.*

## below

If something is **below** another thing, it is under it. *Katy sank **below** the surface of the water.*
■ *opposite* **above**

## belt

**belts**
A **belt** is a thin band of leather, cloth or plastic that you wear around your waist. *Henry's new **belt** is red with a silver buckle.*

## bench

**benches**
A **bench** is a long, hard seat for several people.

## bend

**bends bending bent**
If something **bends**, it changes its shape so that it is not straight. *These straws **bend** in the middle. Janie **bent** over and touched her toes.*

## beneath

If something is **beneath** another thing, it is below it. *Spot is hiding **beneath** the table.*

## bent

If something is **bent**, it is not straight. *The fork was **bent** out of shape.*

## berry

**berries**
A **berry** is a small, soft fruit. Some berries are poisonous.

## beside

If you are **beside** someone or something, you are next to them. *I sit **beside** Sam at school.*

## best

Something that is the **best** is better than all the others. *Jan won a prize for doing the **best** painting.*
■ *opposite* **worst**

## better

1 You use the word **better** to mean very good compared with something else. *My bike is **better** than yours.*
2 If you feel **better**, you do not feel ill any more.
■ *opposite* **worse**

## between

If you are **between** two things, you are in the middle of them. *Kate sat **between** Mike and Sarah.*

## beware

The word **beware** tells you to be careful because something is dangerous. ***Beware** of the bull.*

## bicycle

**bicycles**
A **bicycle** is a vehicle with two wheels. You push the pedals to turn the wheels.

## big

**bigger biggest**
A **big** person or thing is large.
■ *opposite* **small**

Some other words for big are **enormous, gigantic, huge, massive** and **vast.**

20

# bike
**bikes**
Bike is short for **bicycle**.

# bin
**bins**
You put rubbish in a **bin**.

# bird
**birds**
A **bird** is an animal with two wings. Birds have beaks and are covered with feathers. Most birds can fly.

*Toucans are **birds** with very big beaks.*

# birthday
**birthdays**
Your **birthday** is the date that you were born. People give you gifts every year on your birthday.

# biscuit
**biscuits**
A **biscuit** is a small snack. Biscuits are baked in the oven until they are hard.

# bit
**bits**
A **bit** is a part of something, often a small part.

# bite
**bites biting**
**bit bitten**
When you **bite** something, you cut into it with your teeth.

*Tamsin **bit** into a pear.*

# bitter
If something is **bitter**, it has a sharp taste that many people don't like. Orange peel and coffee taste bitter.

# black
**Black** is a colour. The letters in this sentence are black.

# blade
**blades**
A **blade** is the flat, sharp part of a knife that is used for cutting. Scissors have two blades.

# blame
**blames blaming blamed**
If you **blame** someone, you think or say that they have made something bad happen. *Alexander **blamed** his brother for breaking his model aeroplane.*

# blank
A **blank** piece of paper has nothing on it.

## blanket

**blankets**
A **blanket** is a thick cover. You put blankets on your bed to keep you warm.

## bleed

**bleeds bleeding bled**
If you **bleed**, blood comes out of your body. *Jared's nose **bled** when he bumped into the door.*

## blew

**Blew** comes from the word **blow**. *Amy can blow very hard. She **blew** out all the candles on her cake.*

## blind

**Blind** people cannot see.

## blink

**blinks blinking blinked**
When you **blink**, you close and then open your eyes very quickly.

## block

**blocks**
A **block** is a thick piece of something, such as wood or stone. Blocks usually have straight sides. *Building **blocks**.*

## blog

**blogs**
A **blog** is someone's website or web page where they often add new comments, stories or pictures. Blog is short for web log.

## blood

▲ *rhymes with* **mud**
**Blood** is the red liquid inside your body. Your heart pushes blood round your body.

## blow

**blows blowing blew blown**
**1** When the wind **blows**, it moves the air. *The wind has **blown** away dad's newspaper.*
**2** When you **blow**, you push air out of your mouth.

*Amy is **blowing** out all the candles.*

## blue

**Blue** is a colour. The sky on a sunny day is blue.

## blunt

**blunter bluntest**
Something that is **blunt** is not sharp. *A **blunt** knife.*
■ *opposite* **sharp**

## board

**boards**
A **board** is a flat piece of wood or card. *A dartboard.*

# boast
**boasts boasting boasted**
Someone who **boasts** enjoys telling other people about what they have done, or about the things that they own. *Annie is boasting about her new bicycle.*

# boat
**boats**
A **boat** is a vehicle that carries people or things across rivers, lakes or seas. Some boats have engines and some have sails.

# body
**bodies**
The **body** of a person or an animal is every part of them. Your legs, shoulders and head are all parts of your body.

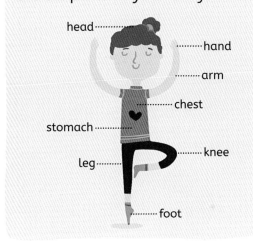

head
hand
arm
chest
stomach
knee
leg
foot

# boil
**boils boiling boiled**
1  When water **boils**, it becomes very hot. There are bubbles in the water and steam rises from it.
2  When you **boil** food, you cook it in boiling water.

# bone
**bones**
Your **bones** are the hard, white parts inside your body. Skeletons are made of bones.

# bonfire
**bonfires**
A **bonfire** is a large fire that is lit outdoors.

# book
**books**
A **book** is a group of pages fixed inside a cover. The pages can have writing or pictures on them.

# boot
**boots**
1  A **boot** is a kind of shoe that covers your foot and part of your leg.
2  The **boot** of a car is the space at the back for carrying things.

## bored

If you are **bored**, you are annoyed because you have nothing to do or because you have to do something you don't want to.

## born

When a baby is **born**, it comes out of its mother.

## borrow

**borrows borrowing borrowed**
If you **borrow** something, someone lets you have it for a short time. *I borrowed Jo's hat.*

## both

**Both** means two together. *Keep both hands on the handlebars.*

## bother

**bothers bothering bothered**
If something or someone **bothers** you, they worry you or annoy you.

## bottle

**bottles**
**Bottles** are containers that hold liquid. They are made from glass or plastic.

## bottom

**bottoms**
1  The **bottom** is the lowest part of something. *The ship sank to the bottom of the sea.*
■ opposite **top**
2  Your **bottom** is the part of your body that you sit on.

## bought

**Bought** comes from the word **buy**. *We always buy Mum a birthday present. Last year, we bought her some flowers.*

## bounce

**bounces**
**bouncing**
**bounced**
When something **bounces**, it springs back after hitting another thing. *Hannah bounced on her big ball.*

## bow

**bows**
▲ rhymes with **low**
1  A **bow** is a knot with two loops. You tie your shoelaces in a bow.
2  A **bow** is also a curved piece of wood with a string stretched from one end to the other. You use a bow to shoot arrows.
3  You also use a **bow** to play the violin or cello. A bow is made from a long piece of wood with hair stretched from one end to the other.

bow

## bowl

**bowls**
▲ *rhymes with goal*
You use a **bowl** to hold food or drink. Bowls are usually round and deeper than plates.

## box

**boxes**
**Boxes** are containers that usually have straight sides.

## boy

**boys**
A **boy** is a male child.

## bracelet

**bracelets**
A **bracelet** is a chain or a band that you wear around your wrist.

## brake

**brakes**
You use the **brakes** on a car or a bike to make it slow down or stop.

## branch

**branches**
A **branch** is part of a tree. Branches grow from the trunk of a tree.

## brave

**braver bravest**
If you are **brave**, you are willing to do something frightening. *Ellie was **brave** about staying in hospital.*

## bread

**Bread** is a food that is made with flour and baked in an oven.

## break

**breaks breaking broke broken**
**1** When something **breaks**, it splits into pieces. *The mug **broke** when Anna dropped it.*
**2** When a machine **breaks**, it stops working. *Toby has **broken** my radio.*

## breakfast

**breakfasts**
▲ *say **brek**-fust*
**Breakfast** is the first meal of the day.

## breathe

**breathes breathing breathed**
When you **breathe**, you suck air into your body and then let it out again. You can breathe through your nose or your mouth.

A B C D E F G H I J K L M N O P Q R S T U V W X Y Z

## breeze

**breezes**
A **breeze** is a light wind.

## brick

**bricks**
A **brick** is a block of baked clay.
Bricks are used for building.

## bridge

**bridges**
A **bridge** is something that is
built over a river, a road or
a railway so that people
can get across.

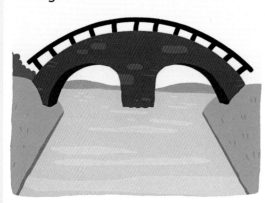

## bright

**brighter brightest**
1 Something that
is **bright** gives out
a lot of light.
*The Sun is very **bright**.*
2 A **bright** colour is strong
and easy to see. *Jemima
wore a **bright** pink jumper.*

## brilliant

Something that is **brilliant** is
very good. *A **brilliant** idea.*

## bring

**brings bringing brought**
If you **bring** something, you take
it with you. *Please **bring** a packed
lunch tomorrow.*

## broad

**broader broadest**
Something that is **broad** is wide.
*The boat drifted down the
**broad**, brown river.*

## broken

**Broken** comes from the word
**break**. *Toby breaks everything.
He's even **broken** Dad's camera.*

## brother

**brothers**
Your **brother** is a boy who has
the same mum and dad as you.

## brought

**Brought** comes from the
word **bring**. *Lucy often brings
something interesting to school.
Last week, she **brought** her
pet snake.*

## brown

**Brown** is a colour. Wood
and chocolate are brown.

## bruise

**bruises**
A **bruise** is a purple mark on your
skin. You get a bruise when part
of your body is hit by something.
*Marc has a **bruise** on his knee
where he knocked it.*

# brush

**brushes**

A **brush** has lots of  hairs or wires fixed to a handle. Toothbrushes, paintbrushes and hairbrushes are types of brush.

# bubble

**bubbles**

A **bubble** is a ball of gas inside a liquid. There are bubbles in boiling water and fizzy drinks. Soap bubbles can float through the air.

# bucket

**buckets**

A **bucket** is a container with a flat bottom and a handle.

# build

**builds building built**

If you **build** something, you make it by fixing things together. *Harry is **building** a castle.*

# building

**buildings**

A **building** is a place with walls and a roof. Houses, shops, schools and offices are buildings.

# built

**Built** comes from the word **build**. *Hannah won our competition to build the tallest tower. She **built** one that was three metres high.*

# bulb

**bulbs**

1 A **light bulb** shines when you turn on a light. Light bulbs are made of glass.
2 A **bulb** is the part of some plants that is under the ground. Flowers such as daffodils and crocuses grow from bulbs.

# bull

**bulls**

A **bull** is a male cow. Bulls are bigger and stronger than female cows.

# bulldozer

**bulldozers**

A **bulldozer** is a large machine that moves rocks and soil.

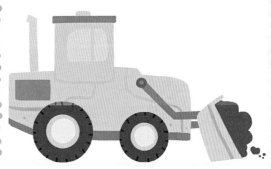

## bully

**bullies bullying bullied**
**Bullying** is trying to hurt or frighten other people.

## bump

**bumps**
A **bump** is something round that sticks out. *Osman has a* **bump** *on his head.*

## bump

**bumps bumping bumped**
If you **bump** into something, you hit it without meaning to. *Osman* **bumped** *into a shelf.*

## bunch

**bunches**
A **bunch** is a group of things. *A* **bunch** *of flowers.* **Bunches** *of grapes.*

## bungalow

**bungalows**
A **bungalow** is a house that only has one level.

## burglar

**burglars**
A **burglar** is someone who gets into a building and steals things.

## burn

**burns burning burned burnt**
**1** If you **burn** something, you set it on fire. *We* **burn** *logs in our fireplace.*
**2** **Burn** also means to damage something with fire or heat. *Alfie has* **burnt** *the toast again.*
**3** If you **burn** yourself, you touch something hot and get hurt.

## burst

**bursts bursting burst**
When something **bursts**, it breaks apart suddenly. *The bag* **burst** *and scattered apples all over the floor.*

## bury

**buries burying buried**
▲ *rhymes with* **very**
If you **bury** something, you put it in the ground and cover it with earth. *The pirates* **buried** *the treasure under a tree.*

## bus

**buses**
A **bus** is a large vehicle that carries lots of people. Buses usually carry people on short journeys between towns or around cities.

## bush

**bushes**

A **bush** is a plant with lots of branches, but no trunk. Bushes are usually smaller than trees.

## busy

**busier busiest**

▲ *rhymes with* **dizzy**

1 **Busy** people have lots of things to do.

2 If a place is **busy**, there is a lot going on, or a lot of people there.

## butcher

**butchers**

A **butcher** is someone who sells meat.

## butter

**Butter** is a yellow food made from milk. You can spread butter on bread or use it for cooking.

## butterfly

**butterflies**

A **butterfly** is an insect with four large wings.

## button

**buttons**

1 A **button** is something that you press to make something work. *Jacob pressed the **button** to turn on the TV.*

2 A **button** is a small object that is sewn onto clothes. Buttons fit into buttonholes to fasten clothes together.

## buy

**buys buying bought**

When you **buy** something, you pay money so that you can have it. *Chloe is **buying** a new dress.*

■ *opposite* **sell**

## cabbage

**cabbages**

A **cabbage** is a vegetable with lots of leaves. Cabbages can be green, white or purple.

## café

**cafés**

▲ *say* **kaf**-*ay*

A **café** is a place that sells food and drink, with tables and chairs where you can sit.

## cage

**cages**

A **cage** is a box or a room with bars. Some pets and zoo animals are kept in cages.

a b c d e f g h i j k l m n o p q r s t u v w x y z

## cake

**cakes**
A **cake** is a sweet food that is baked in an oven. Cakes are made with eggs, flour, sugar and butter.

## calculator

**calculators**
A **calculator** is a machine that gives you answers to sums.

## calendar

**calendars**
A **calendar** is a list of all the days, weeks and months in a year. *Olivia marked her birthday on the* **calendar**.

## calf

**calves**
A **calf** is a baby cow. Baby elephants, giraffes and whales are also called calves.

## call

**calls calling called**
1 If you **call** someone, you shout to them so that they come to you. *Dad* **called** *us to come inside for dinner*.
2 When you **call** someone something, you give them a name. *Tom* **called** *his kitten Pepper*.
3 **Call** also means to telephone. *David* **calls** *his uncle every week*.

## calm

**calmer calmest**
If you are **calm**, you are quiet and not worried.

## came

**Came** is from the word **come**. *Henry comes to stay with us every summer. Last year, he* **came** *in August*.

## camel

**camels**
A **camel** is a large animal with one or two humps on its back. Camels carry people and things across deserts.

## camera

**cameras**
A **camera** is a machine that you use to take photographs.

## camp

**camps camping camped**
When you **camp**, you live in a tent for a short time.

## can

**cans**
A **can** is a metal container with curved sides.

# can

**could**
If you **can** do something, you are able to do it. *Oscar **can** juggle.*
■ *opposite* **cannot**

# canal

**canals**
A **canal** is a man-made river.

# candle

**candles**
A **candle** is a stick of wax with a string through the middle, called a wick. When a candle burns, it shines.

Some words that begin with a "c" sound, such as **kangaroo**, are spelt with a "**k**".

# cannot

If you **cannot** do something, you are not able to do it. *Rebecca **cannot** come.*
■ *opposite* **can**

# canoe

**canoes**
▲ *say kan-oo*
A **canoe** is a narrow, light boat that you move with paddles.

# can't

**Can't** is a short way of saying cannot. *Rebecca **can't** come.*

# cap

**caps**
A **cap** is a soft hat with a peak at the front.

# capital

**capitals**
1 A **capital** is the main city of a country. The leaders of a country work in the capital. *The **capital** of Japan is Tokyo.*
2 A **capital** is also a big letter of the alphabet, such as R or Z. You use a capital when you begin a sentence or write a name. You can see all the capital letters in the strip down the side of the opposite page.

# car

**cars**
A **car** is a vehicle with an engine and four wheels. People drive from place to place in cars.

# caravan

**caravans**
A **caravan** is a small home on wheels. Some caravans can be pulled along by a car.

## card
**cards**
1  **Card** is stiff paper.
2  A greetings **card** is a folded piece of stiff paper. It has a picture on the front and a message inside. You send cards to people at special times, such as birthdays.

3  **Playing cards** are pieces of stiff paper with numbers or pictures on them, used to play games.

## cardboard
**Cardboard** is thick, strong paper. It is used to make boxes.

## cardigan
**cardigans**
A **cardigan** is a knitted jacket. Cardigans fasten at the front.

## care
**cares caring cared**
1  If you **care for** a person or an animal, you look after them. *Harry has two rabbits and he cares for them himself.*
2  If you **care about** something, you think that it is important.

## careful
If you are **careful**, you think about what you are doing and try not to make mistakes.
■ *opposite* **careless**

*Ben was **careful** not to spill the drinks.*

## careless
Someone who is **careless** does not think about what they are doing. *It was **careless** of Fergus to forget his coat.*
■ *opposite* **careful**

## carpet
**carpets**
A **carpet** is a thick, soft covering for a floor.

## carriage
**carriages**
**Carriages** are the parts of a train that contain the passengers.

## carrot
**carrots**
A **carrot** is a long, orange vegetable that grows under the ground. You can eat carrots raw or cooked.

# carry

**carries carrying carried**
If you **carry** something, you take it somewhere with you. *James carried his bag to the station.*

# carton

**cartons**
**Cartons** are containers used to hold food or drink. They are made from card or plastic.

# cartoon

**cartoons**
1 A **cartoon** is a film that uses drawings rather than actors.
2 A **cartoon** is also a funny drawing.

# case

**cases**
You use a **case** to store or carry things. *Ginny keeps her glasses in a case.*

# cash

**Cash** is money in coins or notes.

# castle

**castles**
A **castle** is a big building with high walls to keep enemies out. Most castles were built a long time ago.

# cat

**cats**
A **cat** is a furry animal with a long tail. Cats are often kept as pets. Large, wild cats, such as lions and tigers, are known as big cats.

# catch

**catches catching caught**
1 When you **catch** something, you take hold of it while it is moving or in the air. *Joseph ran to catch the ball.*
2 If you **catch** a bus or a train, you get on it. *David caught the last bus home.*

# caterpillar

**caterpillars**
A **caterpillar** is a small animal that looks like a worm with lots of short legs. Caterpillars turn into butterflies or moths.

# cattle

**Cattle** is a word for cows and bulls. *We saw some cattle in the field.*

# caught

**Caught** comes from the word **catch**. *Joseph ran to catch the ball. He caught it easily.*

## cauliflower

**cauliflowers**
A **cauliflower**
is a round
vegetable.
Cauliflowers have green
leaves and a white centre.

## cause

**causes causing caused**
If something **causes** something
else, it makes it happen. *Running
with scissors can **cause** accidents.*

## cave

**caves**
A **cave** is a large hole in the side
of a cliff or a mountain, or under
the ground.

## CD

**CDs**
A **CD** is a round piece of plastic
with music or information stored
on it. CD is short for compact disc.

Some words that begin
with a "**c**" sound, such as
**keep, kennel, kettle** and
**key**, are spelt with a "**k**".

## ceiling

**ceilings**
▲ *say **see**-ling*
The **ceiling** is the part of a
room that is above your head.
Lights hang from ceilings.

## celebrate

**celebrates celebrating celebrated**
When people **celebrate**, they have
fun together to mark a special
occasion. *We **celebrated** Auntie's
birthday with a big party.*

## celebrity

**celebrities**
A **celebrity** is a famous person,
such as a singer or footballer.

## cellar

**cellars**
A **cellar** is a room under a house,
often used to store things.

## cello

**cellos**
▲ *say **chel**-lo*
A **cello** is
a musical
instrument like
a large violin.

*Rosalind loves
to play the **cello**.*

## cement

**Cement** is a grey powder that is
mixed with water and goes very
hard when it dries. People use
cement to stick bricks together.

## centre

**centres**
The **centre** of something
is the middle of it.

## century

**centuries**
A **century** is a period of one hundred years.

## cereal

**cereals**
**1 Cereal** is a food that you eat for breakfast. Most people eat cereal with milk.
**2 Cereals** are also farm plants such as wheat or rice. Their seeds are used for food.

## certain

If you are **certain** about something, you are sure about it. *Robert is* **certain** *that his team will win.*

## certificate

**certificates**
A **certificate** is a piece of paper that says you have done something. *A cycling* **certificate**.

## chain

**chains**
A **chain** is a row of metal loops that are joined together.

## chair

**chairs**
A **chair** is a seat with four legs and a back. Chairs are made for one person to sit on.

## chalk

**chalks**
A **chalk** is a stick of powdered rock used for drawing. Chalks can be white or coloured.

## champion

**champions**
A **champion** is the winner of a race or a competition.

## chance

**chances**
**1** When you have the **chance** to do something, it is possible for you to do it. *Petra has the* **chance** *to go skiing.*
**2** If there is a **chance** that something will happen, it might happen, or it might not. *There's a* **chance** *it will snow later.*
**3** If something happens **by chance**, it has not been planned.

## change

**Change** is the money given back to you when you hand over more money than something costs.

## change

**changes changing changed**
**1** When something **changes**, it is different from how it was before. *If the weather* **changes***, we'll go back inside.*
**2** When you **change**, you put on different clothes. *Molly* **changed** *before she went out.*

## channel
**channels**
A **channel** is what you choose on a television or radio to see or hear programmes shown by a certain station.

## chapter
**chapters**
A **chapter** is a part of a book.
*The book has 12 **chapters**.*

## character
**characters**
▲ *say **karrak**-ter*
1 A **character** is a person in a story, a film or a play.
2 Your **character** is the sort of person you are.

## charge
If someone is **in charge** of something, they look after it.
*Mrs Parsnip is **in charge** of our class.*

## charge
**charges charging charged**
1 When you **charge** a battery or a phone, you fill up the electricity stored inside it.
2 If someone **charges** you for something, they ask you to pay money for it.

## chart
**charts**
A **chart** is a picture, a map or a list that shows information clearly.

## chase
**chases chasing chased**
If you **chase** a person or an animal, you run after them and try to catch them.
*Finn **chased** Flora.*

## chat
**chats chatting chatted**
When you **chat** to someone you talk to them in a relaxed, friendly way.

## cheap
**cheaper cheapest**
Something that is **cheap** does not cost much.
■ *opposite **expensive***

## cheat
**cheats cheating cheated**
If you **cheat**, you break the rules so that you can win or get something that you want.

## check
**checks checking checked**
If you **check** something, you make sure that it is right.
*Lola **checked** a spelling in her dictionary.*

## cheek
**cheeks**
Your **cheeks** are the soft sides of your face.

## cheer
**cheers cheering cheered**
1 When you **cheer**, you shout happily to show that you like something.
2 When you **cheer** someone **up**, you do or say something to make them feel better.

## cheerful
Someone who is **cheerful** feels and looks happy.

## cheese
**cheeses**
**Cheese** is a food that is made from milk. Cheese can be hard or soft.

## cheetah
**cheetahs**
A **cheetah** is a large wild cat. Cheetahs can run very fast.

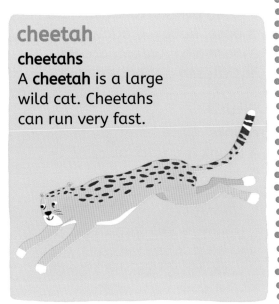

## cherry
**cherries**
A **cherry** is a small, round fruit with a hard seed called a stone in the middle. Cherries can be red, black or yellow.

## chess
**Chess** is a game for two people. You play chess by moving special pieces, such as a queen or a knight, across a board of black and white squares.

## chest
**chests**
1 Your **chest** is the front part of your body between your neck and your stomach.
2 A **chest** is a large, strong box that you keep things in. Chests are usually made of wood.

## chew
**chews chewing chewed**
When you **chew** food, you bite it many times before you swallow it.

## chick
**chicks**
A **chick** is a very young bird.

## chicken

**chickens**
1 A **chicken** is a bird that is kept on a farm.
2 **Chicken** is also the meat that comes from chickens.

37

## chickenpox

**Chickenpox** is a disease. When you have chickenpox, lots of itchy red spots appear on your skin.

## child

**children**
A **child** is a young boy or girl.

## chimney

**chimneys**
A **chimney** is a wide pipe above a fire that carries smoke out of a building. *Our chimney is made of red brick.*

## chimpanzee

**chimpanzees**
A **chimpanzee** is an ape with dark fur. The short name for chimpanzee is chimp.

## chin

**chins**
Your **chin** is the part of your face below your mouth.

## chip

**chips**
A **chip** is a long, thin piece of potato that is either fried in oil or baked.

## choir

**choirs**
▲ *say kwire*
A **choir** is a group of people who sing together.

## choose

**chooses choosing chose chosen**
If you **choose** something, you pick the thing that you want. *Dave is choosing a shirt.*

## chop

**chops chopping chopped**
If you **chop** something, you cut it into pieces.

*Roberto chopped a carrot.*

## chosen

**Chosen** comes from the word **choose**. *Robbie is allowed to choose what we will do. He has chosen a trip to the fair.*

## chunk

**chunks**
A **chunk** is a thick piece of something. *Milo ate a chunk of cheese.*

Some words that begin with a "**c**" sound, such as **kick**, **king**, **kiss** and **kitchen**, are spelt with a "**k**".

## cinema

**cinemas**
A **cinema** is a place where people go to watch films.

## circle

**circles**
A **circle** is a perfectly round shape.

## circus

**circuses**
A **circus** is a show that is held in a big tent.

## city

**cities**
A **city** is a very big place where many people live and work. Cities are usually larger than towns.

## clap

**claps clapping clapped**
When you **clap**, you make a loud noise by slapping your hands together. People clap to show they have enjoyed something, such as a play or a concert.

## class

**classes**
A **class** is a group of people who are taught together. *We are in Mrs Parsnip's class at school.*

## classroom

**classrooms**
A **classroom** is a room in a school where children have lessons.

## claw

**claws**
A **claw** is one of the sharp, curved nails on the feet of some animals. Bears, cats, crocodiles and eagles have claws.

claw

## clay

**Clay** is a kind of earth. When clay is wet, it can be made into different shapes. When it dries or is baked, it becomes hard. *Kate made a pot out of clay.*

## clean

**cleans cleaning cleaned**
When you **clean** something, you take the dirt off it. *Pete needs to clean his boots.*

## clean

**cleaner cleanest**
Something that is **clean** does not have any dirt or food on it. *Raj wore a clean shirt to go to the party. Fetch some clean plates.*
■ *opposite* **dirty**

## clear

**clears clearing cleared**
When you **clear** something, you remove things from it to make space.

## clear

**clearer clearest**
1 If a thing is **clear**, you can see through it. *A **clear** plastic ruler.*
2 Something that is **clear** is easy to understand. *The instructions were **clear** and easy to follow.*

## clever

**cleverer cleverest**
Someone who is **clever** finds it easy to learn and to understand things. *Chen is the **cleverest** girl in our class.*

## cliff

**cliffs**
A **cliff** is the very steep side of a hill, mountain or coast.

cliff

## climb

**climbs climbing climbed**
▲ *rhymes with* **time**
When you **climb** something, you move up it. People sometimes use their hands and feet to climb.

## cloak

**cloaks**
A **cloak** is a loose coat without sleeves.

## clock

**clocks**
A **clock** is a machine that shows you what time it is.

*The **clock** says 11.45.*

## close

**closes closing closed**
▲ *say* **kloze**
If you **close** something, you shut it. ***Close** the door behind you.*
■ *opposite* **open**

## close

**closer closest**
▲ *say* **klose**
If something is **close**, it is near. *Stay **close** to me.*

## cloth

**cloths**
1 **Cloth** is material that is used to make clothes and curtains.
2 A **cloth** is a piece of material that you use to wipe up a mess.

## clothes

**Clothes** are things that you wear, such as shirts, socks and trousers.

# cloud

**clouds**
**Clouds** are white or grey shapes that you see in the sky. They are made of tiny drops of water. Rain, snow and hail come from clouds.

# clown

**clowns**
A **clown** is someone who makes people laugh. Clowns wear make-up and funny clothes and do tricks.

# club

**clubs**
A **club** is a group of people who meet together because they enjoy doing the same thing. *Ali has joined a computer **club**.*

# clue

**clues**
A **clue** is something that helps you to find the answer to a question. *The police need some **clues** to help them find the burglar.*

# clumsy

**clumsier clumsiest**
**Clumsy** people are not very careful about the way they move and often knock things over.

# coach

**coaches**
**1** A **coach** is a large vehicle that carries lots of people. Coaches are mostly used for longer journeys than buses.
**2** A **coach** is also someone who teaches you to play a sport.

# coal

**Coal** is a black rock found under the ground. It burns well, making lots of heat.

# coast

**coasts**
The **coast** is the land next to the sea.

# coat

**coats**
**1** A **coat** is a piece of clothing that you wear over your other clothes. Coats have long sleeves and are usually made from thick material.
**2** An animal's **coat** is the fur or hair that covers its body. *Fido has a long, thick **coat**.*

# cobweb

**cobwebs**
A **cobweb** is an old spider's web, usually found in a dusty corner.

A B C D E F G H I J K L M N O P Q R S T U V W X Y Z

## cockerel

**cockerels**
A **cockerel** is a male chicken.
The short name for cockerel
is cock.

## coffee

**coffees**
**Coffee** is a drink made by
pouring hot water onto the
roasted seeds of the coffee tree.

## coin

**coins**
A **coin** is a small,
flat piece of metal.
Coins are used
as money.

## cold

**colds**
When you have a **cold**, you have
a sore throat and you cough
and sneeze a lot.

## cold

**colder coldest**
**1** If something is
**cold**, it is not
hot or warm.
*A cold drink.*
**2** If the weather
is **cold**, the
temperature is
low. *It was so
cold that Isla
shivered.*
■ *opposite* **hot**

## collar

**collars**
**1** The **collar** of a shirt or a
jacket is the part of it that
fits round your neck.
**2** A **collar** is also a band
that goes round the neck
of a dog or a cat.

## collect

**collects collecting collected**
**1** If you **collect** things, you
keep them as a hobby.
*Sam collects stamps.*
**2** When you **collect** things,
you put them together. *Tilly
collected the empty cups.*
**3** If you **collect** someone,
you take them from a place.
*Dad collected me from school.*

## college

**colleges**
A **college** is a place where
people can learn after they
have left school.

## colour

**colours**
Red, yellow and blue are the
main **colours**. You can make
other colours by mixing
the main ones.

*red*     *yellow*     *blue*

## comb

**combs**

▲ *rhymes with* **home**

A **comb** is a flat piece of plastic or metal with thin teeth. You use a comb to tidy your hair.

## come

**comes coming came come**

When you **come** to a person or a place, you move towards them. *Come here so that I can hear you.*

■ *opposite* **go**

## comfortable

If something is **comfortable**, it feels good. *A comfortable chair.*

## comic

**comics**

A **comic** is a magazine with stories told in pictures.

## common

**commoner commonest**

Things that are **common** are often seen. *Computers are common in schools.*

■ *opposite* **rare**

## compare

**compares comparing compared**

When you **compare** two things, you look at them carefully to see if they are the same or different. *Maisie compared the two dresses to decide which she liked best.*

## compass

**compasses**

**1** A **compass** is something that shows you which way you are facing. A compass has a needle that always points north.

**2** A **compass** is also a tool that you use to draw a circle.

## competition

**competitions**

When you take part in a **competition**, you try to do better than other people. *I came first in the swimming competition.*

## complete

**completes completing completed**

When you **complete** something, you finish it. *Alice completed her homework and went out to play.*

## complete

Something that is **complete** does not have anything missing. *Amy checked to make sure that the jigsaw puzzle was complete.*

## computer

**computers**

A **computer** is a machine that stores words, pictures and numbers, and is often used to go on the internet. *Jake loves playing games on his computer.*

## concentrate

**concentrates concentrating concentrated**
When you **concentrate** on something, you think hard about it. *Akil is **concentrating** on his history project.*

## concert

**concerts**
When people give a **concert**, they play music or sing to an audience.

## concrete

**Concrete** is a mixture of cement, small stones, sand and water. It becomes very hard when it dries. Concrete is used for building.

## confuse

**confuses confusing confused**
If someone **confuses** you, they make it difficult for you to understand something. *Hermione **confused** me with her long words.*

## connect

**connects connecting connected**
If you **connect** two things, you join them together. *Ed **connected** the computer to the printer.*

## consonant

**consonants**
A **consonant** is any letter of the alphabet except the vowels a, e, i, o and u. B and f are consonants.

## contact lens

**contact lenses**
**Contact lenses** are small circles of soft, clear plastic that you put in your eyes to help you see better.

## contain

**contains containing contained**
If a box **contains** something, it has that thing inside it.

## container

**containers**
A **container** is something you use to hold things or keep things in. Boxes, bottles and baskets are all containers.

## continue

**continues continuing continued**
If you **continue** to do something, you don't stop doing it.

## control

**controls controlling controlled**
When you **control** something, you make it do what you want.

*Arthur can **control** his toy car.*

## conversation

**conversations**
When people have a **conversation**, they talk to each other.

## cook

**cooks**
**cooking cooked**
When you **cook** food, you heat it until it is ready to eat.

## cool

**cooler coolest**
Something that is **cool** feels quite cold. *We enjoyed our cool drinks.*

## copy

**copies**
A **copy** is a thing that looks the same as something else. *Jamila liked the painting so much that she made a copy of it.*

## copy

**copies copying copied**
If you **copy** someone, you do the same as they do. *Fergus is copying the way his dad walks.*

## cord

**cords**
**Cord** is a type of string. Some bags have a cord around the top that you pull to close them.

## corner

**corners**
A **corner** is a place where two sides join together. *We met at the corner of the field.*

## correct

**corrects correcting corrected**
If you **correct** something, you make it right where it was wrong.

## correct

If something is **correct**, it does not have any mistakes in it.

## corridor

**corridors**
A **corridor** is a long, indoor passage. *The corridor was full of passengers.*

## cost

**costs costing cost**
If something **costs** an amount of money, that's how much you need to buy it. *How much does that hat cost?*

## costume

**costumes**
A **costume** is a set of clothes that you wear to make yourself look different. *Freddie wore a bear costume for the school play.*

## cot

**cots**
A **cot** is a bed for a baby.
Cots have high sides so the
baby cannot fall out.

## cottage

**cottages**
A **cottage** is a small house.
You often see cottages
in the country.

## cotton

1 **Cotton** is a material that is
used to make clothes. Cotton
comes from the cotton plant.
2 **Cotton** is thread
that you use
for sewing.

## cough

**coughs coughing coughed**
▲ *rhymes with* **off**
When you **cough**, you force
air out of your throat with a
sudden, loud noise. You often
cough when you have a cold.

## could

**Could** comes from the word **can**.
*Oscar can juggle with four balls.*
*Last month, he could only*
*juggle with three.*

## couldn't

**Couldn't** is a short way of
saying **could not**. *Sebastian*
*couldn't swim before he*
*had lessons.*

## count

**counts counting counted**
1 When you **count**, you say
numbers one after the other
in order.
2 When you **count** a number of
things, you add them up to find
out how many there are. *I have*
**counted** *all the jigsaw pieces*
*and there are 30.*

## counter

**counters**
1 A **counter** is a long table in a
shop. Someone stands behind
the counter and serves you.
2 A **counter** is also a small
piece of plastic that you use
in some games.

## country

**countries**
1 A **country** is a part of the
world with its own people
and laws.
2 The **country**, or countryside,
is the land outside towns and
cities. There are fields, woods
and farms in the country.

## courage

▲ *say* **cur**-*idge*
Someone who has **courage**
is brave.

## court

**courts**

**1** A **court** is an area where you play sports. *A tennis court.*

**2** A **court** is a place where a judge and a group of people decide if someone has broken a law or not.

## cousin

**cousins**

▲ *say kuz-un*

Your **cousin** is the son or daughter of your aunt or uncle.

## cover

**covers covering covered**

If you **cover** something, you put something else over it, or all around it. *Monica covered the cake with icing.*

## cow

**cows**

or **cattle**

A **cow** is a large farm animal kept for its milk and its meat.

## crab

**crabs**

A **crab** is a sea creature with a hard shell. Crabs have ten legs and walk sideways.

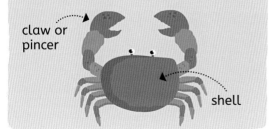

claw or pincer

shell

## crack

**cracks**

A **crack** is a line that shows where something is starting to break. *This mug has a crack in it.*

## cracker

**crackers**

**1** A **cracker** is a thin biscuit. People often eat crackers with cheese.

**2** A **cracker** is a paper tube that bangs when two people pull it apart. Crackers often have something in them, and are pulled at Christmas meals.

## crane

**cranes**

A **crane** is a tall machine that lifts heavy loads.

## crash

**crashes**

**1** A **crash** is a sudden, loud noise. *The plates fell to the ground with a crash.*

**2** A **crash** is also a traffic accident.

## crash

**crashes crashing crashed**

When something **crashes**, it hits something else very hard and makes a sudden, loud noise. *The car crashed into a tree.*

## crawl

**crawls crawling crawled**
When you **crawl**, you move around on your hands and knees. *Jemima **crawled** under the table to hide.*

## crayon

**crayons**
A **crayon** is a coloured pencil. Some crayons are made from wax.

## cream

**Cream** is the thick part of milk. You can use cream in cooking or pour it over puddings and fruit.

## creature

**creatures**
A **creature** is anything that moves and breathes. Horses, lizards, fish, birds and insects are all creatures.

## creep

**creeps creeping crept**
If you **creep** somewhere, you move very slowly and quietly. *Christopher **crept** past his sleeping brother.*

## crew

**crews**
A **crew** is a group of people who work together on a boat or a plane.

## cricket

**Cricket** is a game with a bat and a ball played by two teams. The players have to hit the ball and run up and down the pitch.

## cried

**Cried** comes from the word **cry**. *Poppy began to cry. She **cried** for half an hour.*

## crime

**crimes**
A **crime** is something someone does that is against the law of a country.

## crisp

**crisps**
**Crisps** are very thin slices of potato that are cooked and eaten cold as a snack.

## crocodile

**crocodiles**
A **crocodile** is a large reptile that lives in rivers in hot countries. Crocodiles have sharp teeth, short legs and a long tail.

## crop

corn

**crops**
**Crops** are plants grown in fields and used for food. Wheat, potatoes and corn are crops.

# cross

**crosses**
A **cross** is a sign. It looks like **+** or **X**.

# cross

**crosses crossing crossed**
When you **cross** something, you go from one side of it to the other. *Why did the chicken cross the road?*

# cross

**crosser crossest**
If you are **cross**, you are not pleased about something and you feel angry.

> Some other words for **cross** are **angry, annoyed, irritated** and **furious**.

# crowd

**crowds**
A **crowd** is a large group of people. *A football crowd.*

# crown

**crowns**
A **crown** is a special kind of hat made from gold, silver and jewels. Kings and queens wear crowns.

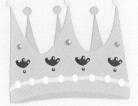

# cruel

**crueller cruellest**
**Cruel** people are unkind and often hurt other people or animals.
■ *opposite* **kind**

# crossword

**crosswords**
A **crossword** is a word puzzle with clues. You work out the answer to a clue, then write the word in squares on the puzzle.

| | | | ¹c | r | ²a | y | ³o | n | |
|---|---|---|---|---|---|---|---|---|---|
| ⁴s | | r | | n | | l | | |
| ⁵m | o | o | | ⁶t | e | d | d | ⁷y |
| o | | w | | s | | | | o |
| ⁸o | i | n | k | | ⁹b | ¹⁰a | n | g |
| t | | | | ¹¹t | | p | | u |
| ¹²h | o | ¹³b | b | y | | ¹⁴a | i | r |
| | | e | | p | | r | | t |
| | ¹⁵d | e | s | e | r | t | | |

a completed crossword

**ACROSS**
1 Coloured pencil
5 Sound of a cow
6 Cuddly toy bear
8 Sound of a pig
9 Loud noise
12 Pastime
14 What you breathe
15 Very dry place

**DOWN**
1 Queen's hat
2 Small insects
3 Not young
4 Not rough
7 A thick food made out of milk
10 Not together
11 Write using a keyboard
13 Insect that makes honey

a b c d e f g h i j k l m n o p q r s t u v w x y z

## crumb

**crumbs**
A **crumb** is a very small piece of dry food. *Cake **crumbs**.*

## crust

**crusts**
The **crust** is the hard part on the outside of a pie or a loaf of bread. *Nathan never eats his **crusts**.*

## cry

**cries crying cried**
When you **cry**, tears come from your eyes. People cry when they are sad or hurt.

## cube

**cubes**
A **cube** is a solid shape with six square sides. Most dice are cubes.

## cucumber

**cucumbers**
A **cucumber** is a long, green vegetable that you eat in salads.

## cuddle

**cuddles cuddling cuddled**
When you **cuddle** someone, you hold them closely in your arms.

## cup

**cups**
You drink from a **cup**. Cups are usually round and often have a handle on one side.

## cupboard

**cupboards**
▲ *say **cub**-erd*
A **cupboard** is a piece of furniture which you keep things in. *Biff put his toys in the **cupboard**.*

## curious

If you are **curious** about something, you want to find out about it. *Edward was **curious** about the parcel.*

## curl

**curls**
A **curl** is a piece of hair that is curved. *Caroline has beautiful **curls**.*

## curtain

**curtains**
A **curtain** is a piece of material that you pull across a window to cover it.

## curve

**curves**
A **curve** is a line that bends.

## cushion

**cushions**
A **cushion** is a soft pad that you use to make sofas and chairs more comfortable.

## customer

**customers**
Anyone who buys something from a shop is a **customer** of that shop.

## cut

**cuts cutting cut**
1 If you **cut** something, you use a knife or a pair of scissors to divide it into pieces. *Mum cut the potatoes into chips.*
2 When you **cut** yourself, something sharp pushes through your skin and makes you bleed.

## cyberbully

**cyberbullies**
A **cyberbully** is someone who uses the internet or a mobile phone to bully people.

## cycle

**cycles cycling cycled**
To **cycle** is to ride a bicycle. *My dad cycles to work every day.*

# Dd

## dad

**dads**
**Dad** is a name for your father.

## daily

If something happens **daily**, it happens every day.

## daisy

**daisies**
**Daisies** are common flowers with white petals and a yellow centre.

## damage

**damages damaging damaged**
If you **damage** something, you spoil it or break it.

## damp

**damper dampest**
Something **damp** is a little bit wet. *The dew has made our lawn damp.*

## dance

**dances dancing danced**
When you **dance**, you move your body to music.

**51**

a b c d e f g h i j k l m n o p q r s t u v w x y z

## danger

You are in **danger** when something could very easily happen to hurt you.

## dangerous

If something is **dangerous**, it can hurt or kill you.

## dare

**dares daring dared**
1 If you **dare** to do something, you are brave enough to do it. *Peter **dared** to jump off the top diving board.*
2 If you **dare** someone to do something, you test them by asking them to do it. *Fiona **dared** James to climb the tree.*

## dark

**darker darkest**
1 When it is **dark**, there is no light or very little light.
2 **Dark** colours are not pale. *Dark blue.*
■ *opposite* **light**

## date

**dates**
When someone asks you what the **date** is, you tell them the day and the month.

*The **date** today is 20th June.*

## daughter

**daughters**
A **daughter** is somebody's female child.

## day

**days**
1 **Day** is the time when it is light outside. *We've been out all **day**.*
■ *opposite* **night**
2 A **day** is a period of 24 hours, starting and ending at midnight. There are seven days in a week. Tuesday and Saturday are days.

## dead

If people, animals or plants are **dead**, they are no longer living.
■ *opposite* **alive**

## deaf

**Deaf** people cannot hear at all or cannot hear very well.

## dear

**dearer dearest**
1 If someone is **dear** to you, you love them. *Rachel is a **dear** friend.*
2 You use the word **dear** when you begin a letter. ***Dear** Mrs Bott.*

## decide

**decides deciding decided**
When you **decide** something, you work out what you're going to do. *Poppy **decided** to wear her purple shorts.*

## deck
**decks**
A **deck** is a floor on a boat or a ship.

## decorate
**decorates**
**decorating**
**decorated**
1 When you **decorate** something, you add things to it to make it look prettier. *Billy* **decorated** *the hall for his party.*
2 If you **decorate** a room, you paint it or put wallpaper on its walls.

## deep
**deeper deepest**
Something that is **deep** goes down a long way. *A* **deep** *well.*
■ *opposite* **shallow**

## deer
**deer**
A **deer** is an animal with four legs and brown fur. Deer live in forests and can run very fast. Male deer have big horns called antlers.

## delicious
Food or drink that is **delicious** tastes or smells very good.

## deliver
**delivers delivering delivered**
If you **deliver** something, you take it to somebody. *The postman* **delivered** *a parcel.*

## dentist
**dentists**
A **dentist** is someone who takes care of your teeth.

## depth
**depths**
The **depth** of a thing is how far it goes down. *We measured the* **depth** *of the pool.*

## describe
**describes describing described**
When you **describe** something, you say what it is like. *Alfie* **described** *his new house to me.*

## desert
**deserts**
A **desert** is a large piece of land where very few plants grow. Deserts are very dry and are often covered with sand.

## deserve

**deserves deserving deserved**
If you **deserve** a thing, you earn it by doing something.
*Eleanor deserves a rest after all her hard work.*

## desk

**desks**
A **desk** is a kind of table that you sit at to write or to do work.

## dessert

**desserts**
A **dessert** is a sweet food that you eat at the end of a meal.
*Evie chose ice cream for dessert.*

## destroy

**destroys destroying destroyed**
**Destroy** means to damage something so badly that it cannot be mended. *The storm destroyed our garden shed.*

## diagram

**diagrams**
A **diagram** is a drawing that shows something in a clear and simple way.

## diamond

**diamonds**
1 A **diamond** is a jewel.
Diamonds are clear and bright.
2 A **diamond** is also a shape with four sides.

## diary

**diaries**
A **diary** is a book in which you write down things that happen to you each day.

## dice

**dice**
A **dice** is a cube with a different number of spots on each side. You use dice in some games.

## dictionary

**dictionaries**
A **dictionary** is a book of words. Dictionaries tell you what words mean and how to spell them.

## didn't

**Didn't** is a short way of saying **did not**. *Harry didn't like the new wallpaper.*

## die

**dies dying died**
When a person, an animal or a plant **dies**, they stop living.

## different

If a thing is **different**, it is not the same as something else.
■ *opposite* **same**

# difficult

If something is **difficult**, you need to try hard to do it.
- *opposite* **easy**

# dig

**digs digging dug**
When you **dig**, you make a hole in the ground. You usually dig with a spade.

# dinner

**dinners**
**Dinner** is a name for the biggest meal of the day.

# dinosaur

**dinosaurs**
**Dinosaurs** were reptiles that lived millions of years ago. Some dinosaurs were bigger than any land animals alive today.

# direction

**directions**
1  A **direction** is the way that you go to get to a place. *The station is in this direction.*
2  **Directions** are pictures and words that show you how to do something. *These directions show you how to make a kite.*

# dirty

**dirtier dirtiest**
If something is **dirty**, it has mud, food, or other marks on it. *Dirty boots.*
- *opposite* **clean**

# disagree

**disagrees disagreeing disagreed**
If you **disagree** with someone, you do not think the same as they do about something. *We disagreed about the album. Jack thought it was good, but I thought it was awful.*
- *opposite* **agree**

# disappear

**disappears disappearing disappeared**
If something **disappears**, you cannot see it any more. *The Sun disappeared behind a cloud.*
- *opposite* **appear**

# disappointed

If you are **disappointed**, you are sad because something has not gone the way you wanted it to. *Jo was disappointed that her friend couldn't come.*

a b c d e f g h i j k l m n o p q r s t u v w x y z

## disaster
**disasters**
A **disaster** is something terrible that happens.

## disco
**discos**
A **disco** is a party with music for dancing. There are often flashing lights at discos.

## discover
**discovers discovering discovered**
When you **discover** something, you find out about it for the first time. *Megan **discovered** that her friend had been lying.*

## discuss
**discusses discussing discussed**
When you **discuss** something, you talk about it with someone else. *We **discussed** which way we would go home.*

## disease
**diseases**
A **disease** is something that makes you ill. Chickenpox is a disease.

## disguise
**disguises**
A **disguise** is something you wear so that people won't recognize you.

## dish
**dishes**
You put food in a **dish**. Dishes are deeper than plates.

## dishonest
▲ *say diss-**on**-ist*
Someone who is **dishonest** does not tell the truth.
■ *opposite* **honest**

## dishwasher
**dishwashers**
A **dishwasher** is a machine that washes and dries plates and dishes.

## dislike
**dislikes disliking disliked**
When you **dislike** something, you do not like it.
■ *opposite* **like**

## disobey
**disobeys disobeying disobeyed**
If you **disobey** someone, you do not do what they tell you to do.
■ *opposite* **obey**

## display
**displays**
A **display** is a group of things that have been arranged for people to look at. *Luca thought the art **display** was brilliant.*

## distance

**distances**
The **distance** between two things is the space between them. *We measured the distance between the tables.*

## disturb

**disturbs disturbing disturbed**
If you **disturb** someone, you stop them doing something for a short time. *Jayden keeps disturbing me when I am trying to read.*

## dive

**dives diving dived**
When you **dive** into water, you jump in head first, with your arms stretched out in front of you.

## divide

**divides dividing divided**
**1** When you **divide** numbers, you find out how many times one number goes into another. *Hans divided 12 by 2.*

$$12 \div 2 = 6$$

■ *opposite* **multiply**

**2** When you **divide** something, you make it into smaller pieces. *Ed divided the cake into six pieces.*

## doctor

**doctors**
A **doctor** is someone who helps sick people to get better.

## doesn't

**Doesn't** is a short way of saying **does not**. *Elsa doesn't mind cold weather.*

## dog

**dogs**
A **dog** is an animal with four legs and a tail, that is often kept as a pet. Dogs come in many shapes and sizes. Some are trained to do work.

## doll

**dolls**
A **doll** is a toy that looks like a person.

## dolphin

**dolphins**
A **dolphin** is a sea animal. Dolphins are clever and playful.

## donkey

**donkeys**
A **donkey** is an animal that looks like a small horse. Donkeys have long ears and a furry coat.

## don't

**Don't** is a short way of saying **do not**. *I don't like strawberries.*

## door

**doors**
You use a **door** to get into a building, a room or a cupboard.

## double

**Double** means twice as much, or twice as many. *Your lolly is double the size of mine.*

## doubt

**doubts doubting doubted**
▲ say **dowt**
If you **doubt** something, you are not sure about it. *I doubted Simon's story.*

## doughnut

**doughnuts**
▲ say **doe**-nut
A **doughnut** is a small cake covered in sugar or icing.

## down

When something moves **down**, it goes from a higher place to a lower place. *We rode our bikes down the hill.*
■ opposite **up**

## download

**downloads downloading downloaded**
When you **download** information, music or a program, you copy it from the internet onto your computer.

## drag

**drags dragging dragged**
If you **drag** something, you pull it along the ground. *Davina dragged her sledge up the hill.*

## dragon

**dragons**
A **dragon** is a fire-breathing monster that you read about in stories. Dragons often have wings and a long tail.

## drain

**drains**
A **drain** is a pipe or tunnel that carries away liquids.

## drama

When you do **drama**, you act or make up plays.

## drank

**Drank** comes from the word **drink**. *Leo likes to drink milk. He **drank** three glasses this morning.*

## draughts

▲ *rhymes with* **rafts**
**Draughts** is a game for two people. You play draughts by moving counters across a board of black and white squares.

## draw

**draws drawing drew drawn**
1 When you **draw**, you use pencils or crayons to make a picture.
2 If you **draw** a game with someone, neither of you wins or loses.
3 When you **draw** curtains, you close them.

## drawer

**drawers**
A **drawer** is a box that slides in and out of a piece of furniture. You use drawers to keep things in.

## drawing

**drawings**
A **drawing** is a picture made with pens, pencils or crayons.

## drawn

**Drawn** comes from the word **draw**. *Laura likes to draw. She has **drawn** a picture of a house.*

## dream

**dreams**
A **dream** is a story that you see and hear while you are sleeping.

## dress

**dresses**
A **dress** looks like a skirt and a top joined together. Women and girls wear dresses. *Erin wore her new **dress**.*

## dress

**dresses dressing dressed**
When you **dress**, you put on your clothes. *Billy **dressed** quickly.*

## drew

**Drew** comes from the word **draw**. *We all had to draw our favourite food. I **drew** a bowl of ice cream.*

## dried

**Dried** comes from the word **dry**. *We hung the clothes outside to dry. They had **dried** by lunch time.*

## drill

**drills**

A **drill** is a tool that makes holes in hard surfaces.

## drink

**drinks drinking drank drunk**

When you **drink**, you swallow liquid.

## drip

**drips dripping dripped**

When something **drips** it falls in drops, or drops fall from it. *The tap is **dripping**.*

## drive

**drives driving drove driven**

When someone **drives** a vehicle, they make it go somewhere.

## drop

**drops**

A **drop** is a tiny amount of liquid. *Drops of rain.*

## drop

**drops dropping dropped**

If you **drop** something, you let it fall, usually by accident. *Daisy **dropped** her dinner on the floor.*

## drove

**Drove** comes from the word **drive**. *Joseph drives a truck. He **drove** thousands of miles last month.*

## drown

**drowns drowning drowned**

If someone **drowns**, they die because they are under water and cannot breathe.

## drum

**drums**

A **drum** is a hollow musical instrument with a thin skin stretched over the end. You hit the skin with sticks or with your hands.

## drunk

**Drunk** comes from the word **drink**. *Fiona drinks tea all the time. She has **drunk** six cups already today.*

## dry

**dries drying dried**

When you **dry** something, you take liquid out of it or off it. *Matilda is **drying** the dishes.*

## dry

**drier driest**

Something that is **dry** does not have any liquid in it or on it.
■ opposite **wet**

## duck

**ducks**
A **duck** is a bird that can swim. Ducks have short legs and can dive underwater.

## dug

**Dug** comes from the word **dig**. *The pirates began to dig. They **dug** a hole to hide their treasure.*

## dull

**duller dullest**
1 A **dull** colour is not very bright.
2 Something that is **dull** is not very interesting. *Ellis thought the story was very **dull**.*

## dungeon

**dungeons**
A **dungeon** is a prison under the ground. Dungeons are usually found in castles.

## dust

**Dust** looks like powder and is made up of tiny, dry pieces of dirt. *The furniture was covered in **dust**.*

## dustbin

**dustbins**
A **dustbin** is a large container with a lid. You put your rubbish in a dustbin.

## duvet

**duvets**
▲ *say **doo**-vay*
A **duvet** is a thick cover for a bed. Duvets are filled with feathers or other soft material.

## DVD

**DVDs**
A **DVD** is a round piece of plastic with a film or information stored on it. *Millie is watching her new **DVD**.*

## dying

**Dying** comes from the word **die**. *Plants die if you do not give them water. Our plants were **dying** when we returned from holiday.*

# Ee

## each

**Each** means every one. *Joel gave **each** puppy a name. The roses cost £1 **each**.*

## eager

If you are **eager** to do something, you really want to do it. *Zach is **eager** to learn the guitar.*

A B C D E F G H I J K L M N O P Q R S T U V W X Y Z

## eagle

**eagles**
An **eagle** is a large bird with a curved beak and sharp claws. Eagles hunt small animals.

## ear

**ears**
Your **ears** are the parts of your body on the sides of your head that you use to hear.

## early

**earlier earliest**
1  If you arrive **early**, you arrive before the time that you were expected. *Sally was **early** because her watch was wrong.*
2  **Early** also means near the beginning of something. *We set off **early** in the morning.*
■ *opposite* **late**

## earn

**earns earning earned**
If you **earn** money, you work to get it. *Clare **earned** some money by working in her uncle's garden.*

## earth

1  **Earth** is another word for soil. Plants grow in the earth.
2  The **Earth** is the planet that we live on.

## earthquake

**earthquakes**
When there is an **earthquake**, the ground shakes and buildings sometimes fall down.

## east

**East** is a direction. The Sun rises in the east.
■ *opposite* **west**

## easy

**easier easiest**
If something is **easy**, you do not have to try hard to do it.
■ *opposite* **difficult**

## eat

**eats eating ate eaten**
When you **eat**, you chew and swallow food. *Simon is **eating** his lunch.*

## echo

**echoes**
▲ *say **ek**-oh*
An **echo** is a sound that you hear again and again. *Our voices made **echoes** in the cave.*

## edge

**edges**
An **edge** is the outside part of something, where it begins or ends. *We walked along the **edge** of the lake.*

## effect

**effects**
An **effect** is a thing that happens because of something else. *Meeting his hero had a powerful **effect** on Ali.*

## effort

If you put **effort** into something, you try hard at it. *Misha has put a lot of **effort** into her project.*

## egg

**eggs**
**Eggs** contain young birds, reptiles or insects, which break out when they are ready to be born. People often eat hens' eggs.

## either

**Either** means one or the other of two. *You can have **either** an apple or an orange.*

## elbow

**elbows**
Your **elbow** is the joint in the middle of your arm, where it bends.

## electricity

**Electricity** is a kind of energy that is used to make light and heat. Electricity is also used to make machines work.

## elephant

**elephants**
An **elephant** is a large, grey animal with a long trunk and two tusks.

## else

1 **Else** means other, or different. *Jamelia decided to try something **else**.*
2 **Else** also means more. *I can't see anybody **else** here.*

## email

**emails**
An **email** is a typed message sent across the internet from one email address to another. It is short for electronic mail.

## emergency

**emergencies**
An **emergency** is a serious problem that happens suddenly. You need to act quickly in an emergency.

## empty

**emptier emptiest**
If something is **empty**, there is nothing inside it.
■ *opposite* **full**

## encyclopedia

**encyclopedias**
An **encyclopedia** is a book that contains information about many different subjects.

## end

**ends**
The **end** of something is its last part. *The end of the story. The end of the train.*

## end

**ends ending ended**
If you **end** something, you finish it. *Leah ended the argument by walking out.*

## enemy

**enemies**
Your **enemy** is someone who hates you and wants to hurt you.

## energy

1  **Energy** is the power that makes machines work and produces heat and light.
2  When you have **energy**, you have the strength to do things.

*Mo is full of energy.*

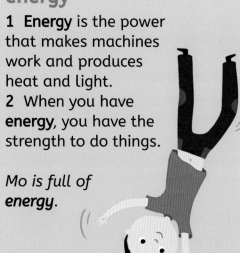

## engine

**engines**
1  An **engine** is a machine that makes things move or work. Cars, planes and ships have engines.
2  An **engine** is also the front part of a train that pulls it along.

## enjoy

**enjoys enjoying enjoyed**
If you **enjoy** something, you like doing it. *Akiko enjoys skating.*

## enormous

Something that is **enormous** is very big. *Whales are enormous.*

## enough

If you have **enough** of something, you have as much as you need. *Have you had enough lunch?*

## enter

**enters entering entered**
When you **enter** a place, you go into it.

## entrance

**entrances**
An **entrance** is a way into a place. *We searched for the entrance to the secret passage.*
■ *opposite* **exit**

## envelope

**envelopes**
An **envelope** is a paper cover for a letter or a card.

## environment

Your **environment** is the land, water and air around you.

## equal

Things that are **equal** are the same. *Mix **equal** amounts of red and blue paint. We both had an **equal** number of sweets.*

## equipment

**Equipment** is a name for the things that you need to do something. Bowls and saucepans are types of kitchen equipment.

## escape

**escapes escaping escaped**
When people or animals **escape**, they get away from somewhere. *The budgie **escaped** from its cage.*

## especially

**1** **Especially** means more than the others. *I **especially** liked the purple hat.*
**2** If something is **especially for** you, it is meant just for you.

## even

**1** An **even** number is a number that you reach when you count in twos. 2, 4, 6 and 8 are even numbers.
■ *opposite* **odd**
**2** Something that is **even** is flat or smooth. *An **even** road.*
■ *opposite* **uneven**

## evening

**evenings**
The **evening** is the part of the day between the afternoon and the night.

## ever

**Ever** means at any time. *Have you **ever** been skating?*

## every

**Every** means all the people or things in a group. *Matt tried **every** chocolate in the box.*

## evil

Someone who is **evil** is very bad and likes to hurt other people.

## example

**examples**
An **example** is a thing that you use to show what similar things are like. *Vikram showed us an **example** of his drawings.*

## except

**Except** means leaving out someone or something. *Everyone* **except** *Oliver enjoyed the play.*

## excited

If you are **excited**, you feel very happy about something and you keep thinking about it. *The night before his birthday, Sam was too* **excited** *to sleep.*

## excuse

**excuses**

An **excuse** is a reason that you give for doing or for not doing something. *Hannah is often late for school, but she always has an* **excuse**.

## exercise

**exercises**
**1** You do **exercise** to keep you fit and strong. Running and swimming are kinds of exercise.

**2** An **exercise** is a short piece of work that helps you to practise something you have learnt. *A* **maths** *exercise.*

## exit

**exits**
An **exit** is a way out of a place.
■ opposite **entrance**

## expect

**expects expecting expected**
If you **expect** something, you think that it will happen.

## expensive

Something that is **expensive** costs a lot of money.
■ opposite **cheap**

## experience

**experiences**
An **experience** is something that you have done or been through. *Going to the zoo was a great* **experience**.

## experiment

**experiments**
An **experiment** is a test that you do to find out something. *We did an* **experiment** *to see which things would float.*

Investigation into floating

| OBJECT | FLOATS | SINKS |
|---|---|---|
| Paperclip | | |
| Coin | | ✓ |
| Leaf | ✓ | ✓ |
| Apple | ✓ | |

## explain

**explains explaining explained**
When you **explain** something, you talk about it clearly so that other people will understand it. *Madhur* **explained** *to her brother how the engine worked.*

## explode

**explodes exploding exploded**
When something **explodes**, it bursts apart with a very loud noise.

## explore

**explores exploring explored**
If you **explore** a place, you look around it for the first time. *The girls **explored** the old house.*

## extinct

If a plant or an animal is **extinct**, there are no more of them alive. *Dodos became **extinct** about 300 years ago.*

dodo

## extra

**Extra** means more than the usual amount. *Ellen had an **extra** cake.*

## extraordinary

Something that is **extraordinary** is very unusual.

## eye

**eyes**
Your **eyes** are the parts of your body that you use to see.

## face

**faces**
Your **face** is the front of your head.

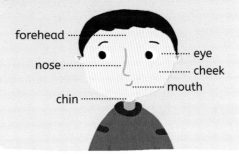

forehead
eye
nose
cheek
mouth
chin

## face

**faces facing faced**
If you **face** something, you look towards it. *Turn to **face** the wall.*

## fact

**facts**
A **fact** is something that is true.

## factory

**factories**
A **factory** is a place where things are made by machines or people. *Cars are made in **factories**.*

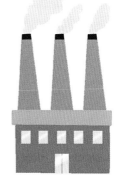

## fade

**fades fading faded**
When a colour **fades**, it gets paler. *My red shirt has **faded** to pink.*

# fail

**fails failing failed**
If you **fail** at something, you are not successful at it. *James searched for his watch, but failed to find it.*

# faint

**faints fainting fainted**
When someone **faints**, they feel weak and dizzy, and often fall over.

# faint

**fainter faintest**
If a noise or a colour is **faint**, it is not very loud or strong. *The baby bird made a faint sound.*

# fair

**fairs**
A **fair** is a place with rides and games where people go to have fun.

# fair

**fairer fairest**
If you are **fair**, you treat everybody by the same rules. If something is fair, it follows the rules. *If I have a sweet, it is fair that you should have one too.*

# fairy

**fairies**
In stories, **fairies** are a kind of tiny people with wings and magical powers.

# fall

**falls falling fell fallen**
When someone **falls**, they suddenly drop to the ground. *Leo fell off the ladder.*

# false

Something that is **false** is not real or not true.

# family

**families**
A **family** is a group of people who live together. Families are usually made up of parents and their children.

# famous

Someone who is **famous** is very well known.

# fan

**fans**
**1** A **fan** pushes air onto you to keep you cool. Some fans you wave with your hand, others are electric.
**2** A **fan** is someone who admires something or someone. *Alex is a football fan.*

## fang
**fangs**
A **fang** is a long, pointed tooth.

## far
**farther farthest**
**Far** means a long way. *My friend has moved far away.*
■ *opposite* **near**

## fare
**fares**
A **fare** is the money that you pay to travel on a bus or a train.

## farm
**farms**
A **farm** is an area of land where farmers grow crops and keep animals.

## farmer
**farmers**
A **farmer** is someone who owns or runs a farm.

## fashion
**fashions**
Clothes that are **in fashion** are popular.

## fast
**faster fastest**
Something that is **fast** can move quickly.
■ *opposite*
**slow**

*A fast car.*

Some other words for **fast** are **quick**, **swift**, **rapid** and **speedy**.

## fasten
**fastens fastening fastened**
When you **fasten** something, you close it up. *Jamal fastened his seat belt.*

## fat
**fatter fattest**
A person or an animal that is **fat** has a big, round body.
■ *opposite* **thin**

## father
**fathers**
A **father** is a man who has a child.

## fault
**fault**
If something bad is your **fault**, you made it happen. *It's Ben's fault that we are late.*

## favour
**favours**
If you do someone a **favour**, you do something helpful for them.

## favourite

Your **favourite** thing is the one you like most of all. *Polly is wearing her **favourite** cap.*

## fear

**Fear** is the feeling you have when you think that something bad might happen. *Jon shook with **fear** as he entered the cave.*

## feather

**feathers**
**Feathers** cover a bird's body and keep it warm. They are very soft and light.

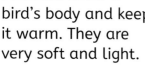

## feed

**feeds feeding fed**
When you **feed** a person or an animal, you give them food. *Vicky never forgets to **feed** her cat.*

## feel

**feels feeling felt**
1 When you **feel** something, you touch it to find out more about it. *Feel how cold my hands are!*
2 If you **feel** happy or sad, warm or cold, that is how you are at the time. *Megan **felt** upset when Alfie left.*

## feeling

**feelings**
A **feeling** tells you how you are or what mood you are in. *A warm, happy sort of **feeling** came over Theo.*

## fell

**Fell** comes from the word **fall**. *Joe often falls when he climbs trees. He **fell** last year and broke his leg.*

## felt

**Felt** comes from the word **feel**. *I feel alright today, but yesterday I **felt** terrible.*

## felt-tip

**felt-tips**
**Felt-tips** are pens with soft tips. They come in many colours.

## female

A **female** person or animal belongs to the sex that can have babies.

## fence

**fences**
A **fence** is an outdoor wall made from wood or wire. *A garden **fence**.*

70

## ferry

**ferries**
A **ferry** is a boat that takes people and cars across water.

## festival

**festivals**
A **festival** is a special day or a special time of the year.

## fetch

**fetches fetching fetched**
When you **fetch** something, you go to it and then bring it back. *Katie **fetched** her book from upstairs.*

## fever

If you have a **fever**, you have a high temperature because you are ill.

## few

If you only have a **few** things, you don't have many of them. *Don't eat my sweets, I've only got a **few**.*

## field

**fields**
A **field** is a piece of land covered in grass, or used to grow crops. Farmers keep animals in fields.

## fierce

**fiercer fiercest**
Something **fierce** is wild and could hurt you. *A **fierce** tiger.*

## fight

**fights fighting fought**
When people **fight**, they try to hurt each other. *The knights **fought** with swords.*

## fill

**fills filling filled**
When you **fill** something, you put so much into it that you cannot add any more.

## film

**films**
When you watch a **film**, you see moving pictures with sounds on a screen. Films are shown in cinemas or on television.

## filthy

**filthier filthiest**
Something that is **filthy** is very dirty. *Sam's boots are **filthy**.*

## fin

**fins**
A **fin** is a thin, flat part that sticks out of a fish's body. Fins help fish to swim.

ABCDEFGHIJKLMNOPQRSTUVWXYZ

# find

**finds finding found**
When you **find** something that you have lost, you see where it is. *Daisy **found** her hamster under the bed.*
■ *opposite* **lose**

# fine

1 When the weather is **fine**, it is dry and often sunny.
2 If you feel **fine**, you feel well and happy.

# finger

**fingers**
Your **fingers** are the long, thin parts at the end of your hand. You have five fingers on each hand. One of these fingers is called a thumb.

# finish

**finishes finishing finished**
When you **finish** something, you come to the end of it. *Lexi quickly **finished** her lunch.*

# fire

**fires**
A **fire** is very hot and bright and is made by burning something.
*The firefighters tried to put out the **fire**.*

# fire engine

**fire engines**
A **fire engine** is a kind of truck that carries firefighters and equipment to put out fires.

# firefighter

**firefighters**
A **firefighter** is someone whose job is to put out fires.

# firework

**fireworks**
When a **firework** is lit, it makes loud noises and flashes of coloured light. Some fireworks shoot up high into the sky.

# firm

**firmer firmest**
Something that is **firm** does not move or change shape easily. *A **firm** mattress is best to sleep on.*

# first

If something is **first**, it comes before everything else. *Henry came **first** in the race.*
■ *opposite* **last**

# first aid

**First aid** is the help that you give people who are hurt or ill before a doctor sees them.

## fish

**fish** or **fishes**

A **fish** is a creature that lives in water. Fish use slits in their sides called gills to breathe under water. *Many different fishes live around coral reefs.*

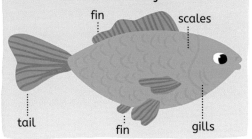

fin

scales

tail

fin

gills

## fist

**fists**

When you make a **fist**, you close your hand tightly.

## fit

**fits fitting fitted**

If something **fits**, it is just the right size. *These jeans fit me perfectly.*

## fit

**fitter fittest**

Someone who is **fit** is healthy. *Jessie runs every day to keep fit.*

## fix

**fixes fixing fixed**

1  If you **fix** something that is broken, you mend it. *Lucas is fixing our radio.*

2  When you **fix** something to another thing, you join them together. *Dad has fixed the shelf to the wall.*

## fizzy

**fizzier fizziest**

A **fizzy** drink has lots of bubbles in it.

## flag

**flags**

A **flag** is a special piece of cloth with coloured shapes on it. Flags are usually attached to the ends of long poles. Each country of the world has its own flag.

Swedish flag

## flame

**flames**

A **flame** is the hot, bright light that comes from something that is burning. *A candle flame.*

## flash

**flashes**

A **flash** is a bright light that starts and stops quickly and suddenly. *A flash of lightning.*

## flask

**flasks**

You use a **flask** to carry drinks. Some flasks keep drinks hot or cold. *Lauren took some orange juice in a flask for her lunch.*

## flat

**flats**

A **flat** is a home on one floor of a building.

## flat

**flatter flattest**
Something that is **flat** does not curve or have any bumps. *A **flat** roof. A **flat** lawn.*

## flavour

**flavours**
The **flavour** of something is what it tastes like. *What **flavour** is your ice cream?*

## flew

**Flew** comes from the word **fly**. *I am going out to fly my new kite. Yesterday, I **flew** it all afternoon.*

## float

**floats floating floated**
1  When something **floats** in water, it stays on the surface.
2  When something **floats** through the air, it moves slowly above the ground.

*The balloon **floated** over the trees.*

## flock

**flocks**
A **flock** is the name for a group of sheep or birds. *A **flock** of starlings.*

## flood

**floods**
▲ *rhymes with* **mud**
A **flood** is a large amount of water that covers ground which is usually dry. *There was a **flood** in our town.*

## floor

**floors**
1  A **floor** is the part of a room that you walk on.
2  A **floor** is also all the rooms on one level of a building. *Jonah lives in a flat on the second **floor**.*

## flour

**Flour** is a powder made from wheat. You use flour to make bread and cakes.

## flow

**flows flowing flowed**
When a liquid **flows**, it moves from one place to another. *The river **flows** through the valley to the sea.*

## flower

**flowers**
A **flower** is part of a plant. Flowers are often brightly coloured and some flowers smell nice.

petal

leaf

stem

## flown

**Flown** comes from the word **fly**. *The baby birds are learning to fly. Some of them have flown away already.*

## flu

If you have **flu**, your body aches and you have a high temperature.

## fly

**flies**
A **fly** is an insect with very thin, clear wings.

## fly

**flies flying flew flown**
When something **flies**, it moves through the air.

## foal

**foals**
A **foal** is a baby horse. *The foal is six months old.*

## fog

**Fog** is thick cloud that is close to the ground. When there is fog, you cannot see very far.

## fold

**folds folding folded**
When you **fold** something, you bend one part of it over another part. *Samantha folded the paper in half.*

## folder

**folders**
1 A **folder** is something you keep pieces of paper in. *A homework folder.*
2 A **folder** is also something you use to store a group of files on a computer.

## follow

**follows following followed**
1 If you **follow** someone, you go behind them.
2 If something **follows** another thing, it happens after it. *Summer follows spring.*

## fond

**fonder fondest**
If you are **fond** of someone, you like them very much.

Some words that begin with an "f" sound, like **phone** and **photograph**, are spelt "ph".

## food

**Food** is what people eat to help them stay healthy and grow.

## foot

**feet**
Your **foot** is the part of your body at the end of your leg.

····· ankle
····· heel
········ big toe
toe  ···· toenail

**75**

## football

**footballs**

1  **Football** is a game played by two teams on a pitch. Each team tries to score goals by kicking a ball into a net.

2  A **football** is the ball used in football games.

## footprint

**footprints**

A **footprint** is the mark made by a foot or a shoe.

## forehead

**foreheads**

Your **forehead** is the part of your face above your eyebrows.

## foreign

Something that is **foreign** comes from another country. *Katy collects **foreign** coins.*

## forest

**forests**

A **forest** is a place where many trees grow close together. Forests are bigger than woods.

## forever

If something goes on **forever**, it never ends. *The talk seemed to go on **forever**.*

## forgave

**Forgave** comes from the word **forgive**. *Ellie found it hard to forgive her sister, but she **forgave** her in the end.*

## forget

**forgets forgetting forgot forgotten**

If you **forget** something, you do not remember it.

## forgive

**forgives forgiving forgave forgiven**

When you **forgive** someone, you stop being angry with them for something they did.

## forgotten

**Forgotten** comes from the word **forget**. *Archie may forget to bring his book. He's **forgotten** it before.*

## fork

**forks**

You use a **fork** to eat. Forks have three or four sharp points called prongs.

## fortnight

**fortnights**

A **fortnight** is two weeks. There are 14 days in a fortnight.

# forwards

If you move **forwards**, you move ahead or towards the front. *Gary ran **forwards** to catch the ball.*

■ *opposite* **backwards**

# fossil

**fossils**
A **fossil** is what is left of an animal or a plant that lived millions of years ago. Fossils are found in rocks.

# foster

**fosters fostering fostered**
When people **foster** a child, the child comes to live with them and becomes part of their family for a short time.

# fought

**Fought** comes from the word **fight**. *My brothers often fight. Yesterday, they **fought** over who would have the last biscuit.*

# found

**Found** comes from the word **find**. *Mum asked me to find my book. I **found** it under the bed.*

# fountain

**fountains**
A **fountain** is a spray of water that is pushed up into the air.

# fox

**foxes**
A **fox** is a wild animal that looks like a dog with reddish fur. Foxes have pointed ears and very thick tails.

# fraction

**fractions**
A **fraction** is a part of a whole thing. Halves and quarters are fractions.

# frame

**frames**
A **frame** fits around the edge of something, like a picture or a window.

a b c d e f g h i j k l m n o p q r s t u v w x y z

## freckles

**Freckles** are light brown spots on your skin. *Ginger's nose is covered with freckles.*

## free

1 If something is **free**, you do not have to pay any money for it.
2 If a person or an animal is **free**, they can go where they like or do what they like.

## freeze

**freezes freezing froze frozen**
When water **freezes**, it becomes so cold that it turns into ice.

## freezer

**freezers**
A **freezer** is a machine that keeps food very cold so that it does not go bad.

## fresh

**fresher freshest**
If food is **fresh**, it has just been made or picked. *Scarlett loves fresh strawberries.*

## fridge

**fridges**
A **fridge** is a machine that keeps food and drinks cool. Fridge is short for refrigerator.

## fried

**Fried** comes from the word **fry**. Fried food has been cooked in hot oil or butter.

## friend

**friends**
▲ *rhymes with* **bend**
A **friend** is someone you like and who likes you. *Archie and his friend enjoy relaxing together.*

## friendly

**friendlier friendliest**
A **friendly** person likes to meet other people and is kind to them.

## frightening

If something is **frightening**, it makes you feel afraid. *The story was so frightening that Maisie couldn't sleep.*

Some other words for **frightening** are **scary, spooky, terrifying** and **petrifying**.

## fringe

**fringes**
Your **fringe** is the hair that hangs down over your forehead.

## frog

**frogs**
A **frog** is a small creature with smooth skin, large eyes and strong back legs that it uses for jumping and swimming.

# front

**fronts**

The **front** of something is the part that faces forwards or comes first. *Karen sat at the front of the bus.*

■ *opposite* **back**

# frost

**Frost** is a thin layer of ice that covers things outside when it is very cold. *Jack scraped the frost off the windscreen.*

# frown

**frowns frowning frowned**

When you **frown**, you push your eyebrows together and wrinkle your forehead. You frown because you are cross or because you are thinking about something.

# frozen

**Frozen** comes from the word **freeze**.

**1** If a pond is **frozen**, the surface of the water has turned into ice.

**2** **Frozen** food is kept very cold so that it does not go off.

# fruit

**fruits**

A **fruit** is the part of a plant that holds the seeds.

apple

watermelon

kiwi fruit

# fry

**fries frying fried**

When you **fry** food, you cook it in hot oil or butter. *Dad fried an egg for his lunch.*

# fudge

**Fudge** is a soft sweet that is made from butter, cream and sugar.

# full

**fuller fullest**

If something is **full**, it cannot hold any more. *The jar is full of biscuits.*

■ *opposite* **empty**

# fumes

**Fumes** are gases that smell bad and make you cough. Cars make fumes.

# fun

When you have **fun**, you have a good time and you are happy.

a b c d e **f** g h i j k l m n o p q r s t u v w x y z

## funny

**funnier funniest**
1 If something is **funny**, it makes you laugh. *A **funny** joke.*
2 **Funny** also means strange or peculiar. *We heard a **funny** noise coming from the attic.*

## fur

**Fur** is the soft hair that covers some animals' bodies. *Polar bears have thick, white **fur**.*

## furious

If you are **furious**, you are very angry. *Sophie was **furious** that her watch had been stolen.*

## furniture

**Furniture** is the name for all the big things, like tables, chairs and beds, that people have in their houses. *When we moved house, we bought some new **furniture**.*

## fuss

**fusses fussing fussed**
When you **fuss**, you worry about something more than you need to. *Mum is always **fussing** about my clothes.*

## fussy

If someone is **fussy**, they are hard to please.

## future

The **future** is the time that has not happened yet. *In the **future**, we might have robots to look after us.*

# Gg

## gallop

**gallops galloping galloped**
When a horse **gallops**, it runs very fast.

*Fury **galloped** away.*

## game

**games**
A **game** is something that you play. Games have rules. Football and draughts are games.

## gang

**gangs**
A **gang** is a group of people who do things together.

## gap
**gaps**
A **gap** is a space between two things. *Marcus has a gap between his two front teeth.*

## garage
**garages**
1  A **garage** is a building where a car is kept.
2  **Garages** are also places where people get their cars mended.

## garden
**gardens**
A **garden** is a piece of land near a house where people grow grass, flowers and other plants.

## gas
**gases**
A **gas** is very light and usually cannot be seen. The air is made of gases. Some gases burn easily and are used in ovens and fires.

## gate
**gates**
A **gate** is a kind of door in a fence, wall or hedge.

## gave
**Gave** comes from the word **give**. *I want to give my dad a present. Last year I only gave him a card.*

## generous
A **generous** person likes to help people and give them things. *It was very generous of Uncle Bill to buy me a bicycle.*

## gentle
**gentler gentlest**
When you are **gentle**, you are careful and kind. *Rosa is gentle with her baby sister.*

## gerbil
**gerbils**
A **gerbil** is a small, furry animal with long back legs. People often keep gerbils as pets.

## germ
**germs**
A **germ** is a tiny living thing that can make you ill. You need a microscope to see germs. *Cover your mouth when you cough, so that you don't spread your germs.*

## ghost
**ghosts**
A **ghost** is a person who has died who some people think they can see.

a b c d e f g h i j k l m n o p q r s t u v w x y z

## giant

**giants**

A **giant** is a very big person that you read about in stories. *The giant bent down and picked up the man.*

## gift

**gifts**

A **gift** is something special you give to someone. *We wrapped Yasmin's gift carefully.*

## giggle

**giggles giggling giggled**

When you **giggle**, you laugh in a silly way. *Alice kept giggling at her dad's new shorts.*

## giraffe

**giraffes**

A **giraffe** is an animal with a very long neck and long legs. Giraffes live in herds and are the tallest animals in the world.

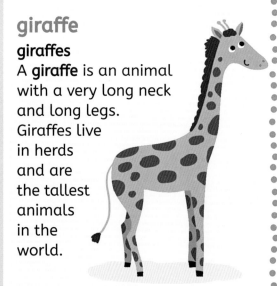

## girl

**girls**

A **girl** is a female child or a young woman.

## give

**gives giving gave given**

1 If you **give** something to someone, you hand it to them. *Anna gave the dice to Reuben.*

2 When you **give** something to someone, you let them have it to keep. *Phoebe loves giving presents to her friends.*

## glad

When you are **glad**, you are pleased and happy about something. *I'm glad you are feeling better.*

## glass

**glasses**

1 **Glass** is a hard material that you can see through. Windows and bottles are made of glass. It is quite easy to break glass.

2 A **glass** is a container that you drink from. Glasses are made from glass. *Dan poured some juice into his glass.*

## glasses

People wear **glasses** to help them see better. Glasses have a frame that holds two special lenses in front of your eyes.

## glove

**gloves**

**Gloves** are clothes that you wear on your hands to keep them warm or to protect them.

## glue

**Glue** is something you use to stick things together. You use glue to make things or to mend things that are broken.

## go

**goes**

If you have a **go** at something, you try doing it, or take a turn at doing it. *Noah wanted to have a go at sailing.*
*It's your go next.*

## go

**goes going went gone**

**1** When you **go**, you move from one place to another, or you leave. *We're going to the park. Let's go!*

■ *opposite* **come**

**2** You use **going to** for something that will happen. *Ben is going to be eight next week.*

## goal

**goals**

You score a **goal** by kicking, hitting or throwing a ball into a net.

## goat

**goats**

A **goat** is an animal with horns and a short tail. Most goats have beards.

## gold

**Gold** is a yellow metal that is very valuable. *A gold ring.*

## goldfish

**goldfish**

A **goldfish** is a small, orange fish. People often keep goldfish as pets.

## gone

**Gone** comes from the word **go**. *Let's go to the park. The others have gone there already.*

## good

**better best**

**1** If something is **good**, you like it. *A good book.*

**2** **Good** people do what is right.

**3** **Good** work is work that has been done well.

■ *opposite* **bad**

Some other words for **good** are **marvellous, fantastic, great** and **terrific**.

## goodbye

You say **goodbye** when someone goes away.

## goose

**geese**

A **goose** is a large bird with a long neck. Geese can swim and fly.

## grab

**grabs grabbing grabbed**
If you **grab** something, you pick it up in a quick, rough way. *Jacob grabbed his bag and ran.*

## gradual

If something is **gradual**, it happens slowly. *A gradual change.*

## grain

**grains**
1 A **grain** of something, such as sand or salt, is a tiny piece of it.
2 A **grain** is also a seed, such as a grain of rice, or a grain of wheat.

## grandfather

**grandfathers**
Your **grandfather** is the father of your mother or your father. Children often call their grandfather grandpa or grandad.

## grandmother

**grandmothers**
Your **grandmother** is the mother of your mother or your father. Children often call their grandmother granny or grandma.

## grape

**grapes**
A **grape** is a small, round fruit that grows in bunches. Grapes are green or purple.

## grapefruit

**grapefruits**
A **grapefruit** is a large, round fruit with a thick skin. It is yellow or pink and has a sour taste.

## grass

**grasses**
**Grass** is a plant with thin, green leaves. Grass grows in fields and gardens.

## grateful

If you are **grateful**, you want to thank someone for something they have done.

## gravy

**Gravy** is a hot, brown sauce that you eat with meat.

## graze

**grazes grazing grazed**
1 If you **graze** your skin, you scrape it against something. *I grazed my elbow on the wall and made it bleed.*
2 When animals **graze**, they eat grass that is growing in a field.

## great

**greater greatest**

▲ say **grate**

**1 Great** means large. *The trees grew to a **great** height.*

**2 Great** also means very important. *Nelson Mandela was a **great** man.*

**3 Great** also means very good. *We had a **great** holiday.*

## greedy

**greedier greediest**

**Greedy** people want more of something than they need. *Augustus was so **greedy** that he ate five bowls of ice cream.*

## green

**Green** is the colour that you make when you mix blue and yellow. Grass is green.

## greenhouse

**greenhouses**

A **greenhouse** is a building with a glass roof and walls. People grow plants in greenhouses.

## grew

**Grew** comes from the word **grow**. *Sunflowers grow very fast. Last week, ours **grew** five centimetres.*

## grey

**Grey** is the colour that you make when you mix black and white. Rain clouds are grey.

## grin

**grins**

A **grin** is a big smile.

## grip

**grips gripping gripped**

If you **grip** something, you hold onto it tightly. *I **gripped** the bat.*

## ground

The **ground** is the surface that you walk on outside.

## group

**groups**

A **group** is a number of people or things that are together or are the same in some way.

## grow

**grows growing grew grown**

When something **grows**, it gets bigger. *John's sunflower has **grown** bigger than May's.*

**85**

## growl

**growls growling growled**
When a dog **growls**, it makes a long, low sound in its throat. *Fido **growled** every time the cat came near.*

## grown

**Grown** comes from the word **grow**. *My auntie is amazed at the way I grow. She says I have **grown** five centimetres since the summer.*

## grown-up

**grown-ups**
A **grown-up** is someone who is no longer a child.

## grumble

**grumbles grumbling grumbled**
If you **grumble**, you keep on saying that you are not happy or that you do not like something.

## guard

**guards guarding guarded**
If you **guard** something, you watch it carefully to keep it safe.

## guess

**guesses guessing guessed**
If you **guess**, you give an answer to something without being sure it is right. *Sam tried to **guess** how many sweets were in the jar.*

## guest

**guests**
A **guest** is someone who comes to visit you. *We have **guests** coming to dinner tonight.*

## guilty

**guiltier guiltiest**
If you are **guilty** of something bad, you made it happen.

## guinea pig

**guinea pigs**
A **guinea pig** is a small, furry animal with no tail. People often keep guinea pigs as pets.

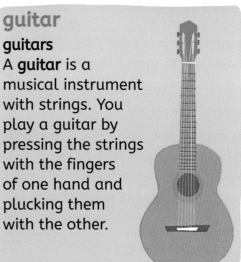

## guitar

**guitars**
A **guitar** is a musical instrument with strings. You play a guitar by pressing the strings with the fingers of one hand and plucking them with the other.

## gum

**gums**
**1** Your **gums** are the firm, pink skin around your teeth.
**2** **Gum** is a kind of sweet that you chew, but do not swallow.

## gun
**guns**
A **gun** is a weapon that is used to shoot something.

## gymnastics
**Gymnastics** are exercises that you do to make you fit and strong. *James is practising gymnastics.*

# Hh

## habit
**habits**
A **habit** is something that you do often, usually without thinking about it. *Hayley's worst habit is biting her nails.*

## had
**Had** comes from the word **have**. *We often have fish for dinner. We had it twice last week.*

## hadn't
**Hadn't** is a short way of saying **had not**. *Natasha hadn't slept very well.*

## hail
**hails hailing hailed**
When it **hails**, small pieces of frozen rain fall from the sky. *It is hailing on my umbrella.*

## hair
**hairs**
**Hair** is what grows on your head and on many animals' bodies. *Rachel has very long hair.*

## half
**halves**
A **half** is one of two parts of equal size that together make the whole of something. *Amelie cut her apple into halves.*

## hall
**halls**
1 A **hall** is a room with other rooms coming off it.
2 A **hall** is also a large room that is used for meetings or plays.

## ham
**Ham** is a type of meat that comes from pigs.

## hammer
**hammers**
A **hammer** is a tool that you use for hitting nails. It has a handle and a heavy metal end.

# hamster

**hamsters**
A **hamster** is a small, furry animal that looks like a mouse. Hamsters have short tails and store food in their cheeks. They are often kept as pets.

# hand

**hands**
Your **hand** is the part of your body at the end of your arm. You use your hand to hold things.

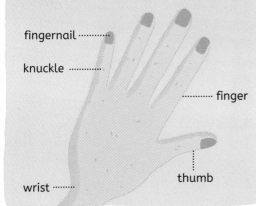

fingernail ·············
knuckle ·············
············· finger
thumb
wrist ········

# hand

**hands handing handed**
If you **hand** something to someone, you place it in their hands. *Please **hand** me a brush.*

# handbag

**handbags**
A **handbag** is a bag used to carry money and other small things.

# handle

**handles**
You use a **handle** to hold something or to move something. *The **handle** on my suitcase is broken. Sophie turned the door **handle** slowly.*

# handsome

Men and boys who are **handsome** are good-looking.

# handwriting

Your **handwriting** is the way that you write letters and words. *Harley has beautiful **handwriting**.*

# hang

**hangs hanging hung**
If you **hang** something, you fix it somewhere above the ground. *Granny **hung** the washing on the line.*

# happen

**happens happening happened**
When something **happens**, it takes place. *What **happens** at the end of the book?*

# happy

**happier happiest**
When you are **happy**, you feel pleased about things.
■ *opposite* **sad**

> Some other words for **happy** are **glad**, **cheerful**, **pleased** and **delighted**.

## harbour
**harbours**
A **harbour** is a safe place where boats can be tied up.

## hard
**harder hardest**
1  Something that is **hard** is firm and solid. *A **hard** bed.*
■ *opposite* **soft**
2  If something is **hard**, it is difficult to do or to understand. *This homework is too **hard**!*

## hard
**harder hardest**
If you do something **hard**, you do it with a lot of energy. *Biff hit him really **hard**. The teacher says you must try **harder**.*

## harmful
If something is **harmful**, it could hurt you or make you ill.

## harvest
**harvests**
**Harvest** is the time when crops are cut or picked.

## has
**Has** comes from the word **have**. *Adam will have a party for his birthday. He **has** one every year.*

## hasn't
**Hasn't** is a short way of saying **has not**. *Oscar **hasn't** arrived yet.*

## hat
**hats**
A **hat** is something that you wear on your head.

## hatch
**hatches hatching hatched**
When an egg **hatches**, a baby bird or animal breaks out of it.
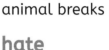

## hate
**hates hating hated**
If you **hate** something, you really do not like it at all. *Mark **hates** cabbage.*

## haunted
If a place is **haunted**, people think that there are ghosts in it.

## have
**has having had**
1  If you **have** something, it is yours. *I **have** a new bicycle. Sarah **has** a cold.*
2  If you **have to** do something, you need to do it. *I **have to** do my homework.*

## haven't

**Haven't** is a short way of saying **have not**. *We haven't got any money.*

## head

**heads**
1 Your **head** is the part of your body where your hair, ears, eyes, mouth and nose are. Your brain is inside your head.
2 The **head** of something is the person in charge. *The head of a school.*

## heal

**heals healing healed**
When a cut **heals**, it gets better.

## healthy

**healthier healthiest**
1 A **healthy** person is well and strong.
2 Something that is **healthy** is good for you. *I try to eat healthy food, such as fruit and vegetables.*

## heap

**heaps**
A **heap** is an untidy pile of things. *Samir left his clothes in a heap on the floor.*

## hear

**hears hearing heard**
When you **hear**, you notice sounds with your ears.

## heart

**hearts**
▲ *rhymes with* **part**
1 Your **heart** is the part of your body that pushes blood around your body.
2 A **heart** is also this shape: It stands for love.

## heat

**heats heating heated**
When you **heat** something, you make it warmer. *Anna heated the soup in a saucepan.*

## heavy

**heavier heaviest**
Something that is **heavy** weighs a lot. *Kenton tried to lift the heavy suitcase.*
■ *opposite* **light**

## he'd

1 **He'd** is a short way of saying **he had**. *He'd always wanted to ride an elephant.*
2 **He'd** is also a short way of saying **he would**. *Tyler says he'd love to go.*

## hedge

**hedges**
A **hedge** is a row of bushes that make a kind of wall. You often see hedges around fields.

# hedgehog

**hedgehogs**
A **hedgehog** is a small animal with lots of spikes on its back. When hedgehogs are frightened, they curl into a ball.

# heel

**heels**
Your **heel** is the back part of your foot.

# height

**heights**
▲ *rhymes with* **light**
Your **height** is how tall you are. *Kate checked Leo's height to see how much he'd grown.*

# held

**Held** comes from the word **hold**. *Henry offered to hold the ladder for his dad. He **held** it until his arms ached.*

# helicopter

**helicopters**
A **helicopter** is an aircraft without wings. It has blades on top that spin around to make it fly or hover.

# he'll

**He'll** is a short way of saying **he will**. *James is finishing his lunch. **He'll** be here soon.*

# hello

You say **hello** when you meet someone.

# helmet

**helmets**
A **helmet** is a hard hat that you wear to protect your head. *Nadia is wearing her bicycle **helmet**.*

# help

**helps helping helped**
If you **help** someone, you do something for them, or you do it with them to make it easier. *Lauren **helped** her dad to put up the tent.*

# helpful

A **helpful** person often helps other people.

# hen

**hens**
A **hen** is a female chicken. Hens are kept on farms for their eggs.

# herd

**herds**
A **herd** is a large group of animals such as cattle, deer or elephants.

# here

**Here** means the place where you are. *I've lived **here** for six years.*
- *opposite* **there**

# here's

**Here's** is a short way of saying **here is**. ***Here's** today's newspaper.*

# hero

**heroes**
A **hero** is someone who is very brave. Stories are often about heroes.

# hers

If something belongs to a girl or a woman, then it is **hers**. *The doll is **hers**.*

# herself

**Herself** means her and nobody else. *Emily has hurt **herself**.*

# he's

**1** **He's** is a short way of saying **he is**. *I'm waiting for Kai to arrive. **He's** coming at two o'clock.*
**2** **He's** is also short for **he has**. ***He's** actually done it.*

# hibernate

**hibernates hibernating hibernated**
When animals **hibernate**, they sleep through the winter. They hibernate to stay alive when it is cold and there is not much food.

# hiccup

**hiccups**
When you have **hiccups**, you keep making a sudden sound in your throat.

# hide

**hides hiding hid hidden**
**1** When you **hide** something, you put it where no one can see it. *Zak **hid** the present under the bed.*
**2** If you **hide** your feelings, you keep them secret. *Lola **hid** her disappointment.*

# high

**higher highest**
**1** Something that is **high** is a long way from the ground. *A **high** tower.*
**2** **High** also means bigger than usual. ***High** prices.*
**3** A **high** voice goes up a long way. Girls and young boys have high voices when they sing.
- *opposite* **low**

# hill

**hills**
A **hill** is a high piece of land. Hills are not as tall as mountains.

# himself

**Himself** means him and nobody else. *Max has hurt **himself**.*

# hippopotamus

**hippopotamuses**
A **hippopotamus** is a large animal with short legs and thick skin. Hippopotamuses live in and around rivers.

# his

If something belongs to a boy or a man, then it is **his**.
*The ball is **his**.*

# history

**History** is the story of what has happened in the past.

# hit

**hits hitting hit**
When two things **hit** each other, they come together very hard.
*The car **hit** a wall.*
*Peter **hit** his head.*

# hobby

**hobbies**
A **hobby** is something you enjoy doing in your spare time. *Jon's **hobby** is collecting badges.*

# hold

**holds holding held**
**1** If you **hold** something, you have it in your hands or your arms. *Liz **held** the kitten gently.*
**2** **Hold** also means to have room for something. *This jug **holds** two litres. The hall **holds** about two hundred people.*

Some words that begin with an "**h**" sound, such as **whole**, are spelt "**wh**".

# hole

**holes**
A **hole** is a gap or a hollow place. *I see a **hole** in your shirt. The workers dug a **hole** in the road.*

# holiday

**holidays**
A **holiday** is a time when you do not have to work or go to school. People often spend their holidays away from home.

# hollow

Something that is **hollow** has an empty space inside it.
*We crawled through the **hollow** log.*

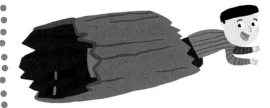

## home

**homes**
Your **home** is the place where you live. *We are going to stay at **home** today.*

## homework

**Homework** is work that a teacher gives you to do at home.

## honest

Someone who is **honest** tells the truth and can be trusted.
■ *opposite* **dishonest**

## honey

**Honey** is a sweet, sticky food that is made by bees. You can eat honey on bread.

## hood

**hoods**
The **hood** of a coat is the part that covers your head.

*As soon as it started to rain, Ruth put up her **hood**.*

## hoof

**hooves**
An animal's **hoof** is the hard part of its foot. Horses, deer and cows have hooves.

## hook

**hooks**
A **hook** is a curved piece of metal or plastic. Some hooks are used for hanging things up. Other hooks are used for catching things, like fish.

## hop

**hops hopping hopped**
1 When you **hop**, you jump on one foot.
2 When birds and rabbits **hop**, they jump forwards with their feet close together.

## hope

**hopes hoping hoped**
If you **hope** something, you want it to happen and think that it might. *I **hope** we'll go to the seaside tomorrow.*

## horn

**horns**
1 A **horn** is one of the hard, pointed bones that grow out of some animals' heads. Goats and bulls have horns.
2 A **horn** is also a musical instrument that you blow. *Gabe enjoyed playing his French **horn**.*

## horrible

Something that is **horrible** is awful or frightening. *That soup was **horrible**. In my dream, I was chased by a **horrible** monster.*

## horse

**horses**
A **horse** is a large animal with four legs and a long tail. People ride horses.

bridle
mane
saddle
reins
stirrup
hoof

## hose

**hoses**
A **hose** is a long, narrow tube made of rubber or plastic. People use hoses to put water on gardens.

## hospital

**hospitals**
A **hospital** is a building where people who are ill or hurt are looked after. Doctors and nurses work in hospitals.

## hot

**hotter hottest**
Something that is **hot** has a high temperature.
*Be careful, the drink is **hot**.*
■ *opposite* **cold**

## hotel

**hotels**
A **hotel** is a big building with many bedrooms and a restaurant. People pay to stay in hotels when they are away from home.

## hour

**hours**
An **hour** is an amount of time. There are 60 minutes in an hour, and 24 hours in a day.

## house

**houses**
A **house** is a building that people live in. *Where is your **house**?*

## hover

**hovers hovering hovered**
When something **hovers**, it stays in one place in the air.

*The hummingbird **hovered** in front of the flower.*

## how

1 **How** means in what way. *How do I turn off the computer?*
2 You also use **how** when you ask about an amount. *How much money do you have? How many people are coming to the play?*

h

## how's

**1** **How's** is a short way of saying **how is**. *How's your brother feeling today?*
**2** **How's** is also short for **how has**. *How's he managed that?*

## hug

**hugs hugging hugged**
When you **hug** someone, you hold them tightly in your arms. *Gary hugged Mario when he scored the final goal.*

## huge

Something **huge** is very big. *Whales are huge.*

## human being

**human beings**
A **human being** is a person. Men, women and children are all human beings.

## hump

**humps**
A **hump** is a big, rounded lump. Camels have humps on their backs.

## hung

**Hung** comes from the word **hang**. *Christopher decided to hang up the picture. He hung it in his room.*

## hungry

**hungrier hungriest**
If you are **hungry**, you want to eat something.

## hunt

**hunts hunting hunted**
**1** When animals **hunt**, they chase another animal, then kill it and eat it.
**2** If you **hunt for** something, you look for it carefully. *Tony hunted everywhere for his other sock.*

## hurry

**hurries hurrying hurried**
When you **hurry**, you do something quickly. *Hannah hurried to catch the bus.*

## hurt

**hurts hurting hurt**
If something **hurts** you, you feel pain. *Keira's elbow hurt where she had hit it.*

## husband

**husbands**
Someone's **husband** is the man they are married to.

## hut

**huts**
A **hut** is a small building. Huts can be made from wood, metal, mud or grass.

# hutch

**hutches**

A **hutch** is a kind of cage made from wood and wire. People keep rabbits and other small pets in hutches.

# ice

**Ice** is frozen water. It is very cold, and hard. *The pond was covered in ice.*

# iceberg

**icebergs**

An **iceberg** is a very large piece of ice that floats in the sea.

# ice cream

**Ice cream** is a sweet, frozen food made from milk or cream. There are many different flavours of ice cream.

# icicle

**icicles**

An **icicle** is a long, thin stick of ice. Icicles are made from dripping water which has frozen.

# icing

**Icing** is used to cover cakes. It is made from sugar mixed with water or butter. *Wayne covered the cake with icing.*

# icon

**icons**

An **icon** is a small picture that you click on to start a computer program or open an app.

# I'd

1 **I'd** is a short way of saying **I had**. *I'd already eaten supper by the time William came.*
2 **I'd** is also a short way of saying **I would**. *I'd love to come to your birthday party.*

# idea

**ideas**

1 An **idea** is a thought, or a picture in your mind.
2 If you have an **idea**, you think of something to do, or a way of doing it. *Dylan had lots of ideas for a story.*

A B C D E F G H I J K L M N O P Q R S T U V W X Y Z

## identical

If two things are **identical**, they are exactly the same. *Holly and Vashti have **identical** umbrellas.*

## I'll

**I'll** is a short way of saying **I will**. *I'll be home before it gets dark.*

## ill

When you are **ill**, you are not well. *Nathan was **ill**, so he had to stay in bed.*

## I'm

**I'm** is a short way of saying **I am**. *I'm feeling happy today.*

## imagine

**imagines imagining imagined**
If you **imagine** something, you have a picture of it in your mind. *Esme **imagined** what it would be like to meet a dragon.*

## immediately

If you do something **immediately**, you do it now. *Go to your room **immediately**!*

## impatient

If somebody is **impatient**, they get annoyed if they have to wait.
- *opposite* **patient**

## important

If something is **important**, it matters a lot. *It is **important** to clean your teeth every day.*

## impossible

If something is **impossible**, it cannot be done. *It is **impossible** to control the weather.*
- *opposite* **possible**

## impress

**impress impressing impressed**
If something or someone **impresses** you, you think they are very good. *Isaac was very **impressed** by Ben's magic trick.*

## improve

**improves improving improved**
If something **improves**, it gets better. *My cooking has **improved** a lot this year.*

## in

1 **In** means not outside.
- *opposite* **out**
2 **In** also shows when something is going to happen. *I'll be back **in** an hour.*

## indoors

If you are **indoors**, you are inside a building.
- *opposite* **outdoors**

## infant

**infants**
An **infant** is a baby or a very young child.

## infectious

If a disease is **infectious**, you can catch it from another person.

## inflate

**inflates inflating inflated**
If you **inflate** something, you fill it with air, or another gas. *Dad inflated the air mattress.*

## information

If you ask for **information** about something, you want to find out about it. *I'm looking for information about judo classes.*

## ingredient

**ingredients**
An **ingredient** is one of the things that goes into food. *Katie bought the ingredients for her cake.*

cake ingredients

## initial

**initials**
An **initial** is the first letter of a word or a name. *Edward Thompson's initials are E.T.*

## injure

**injures injuring injured**
If something **injures** you, it harms you. *Libby injured her back when she fell off a stool.*

## ink

**inks**
Ink is a coloured liquid that is used for writing or printing.

## insect

**insects**
An **insect** is a small creature with six legs. Most insects have wings.

dragonfly

## inside

1 If something is **inside** a thing, it is in it. *A plum has a stone inside it.*
2 **Inside** also means indoors. *We went inside when it began to rain.*

## instead

**Instead** means in place of something else. *Leon caught the bus instead of walking home.*

## instructions

**Instructions** are words or pictures that show you how to do something. *Read the instructions before you make the model.*

## instrument

**instruments**

**1** An **instrument** is something that helps you to do a job. *Doctors and dentists use instruments.*

**2** An **instrument** is also something that you use to make music. *Pianos, guitars and horns are all instruments.*

horn

## intelligent

An **intelligent** person finds it easy to learn and understand things.

## interesting

If you find something **interesting**, you want to know more about it.

## internet

The **internet** is a way for computers all around the world to share words, pictures, videos and music.

## interrupt

**interrupts interrupting interrupted**

If you **interrupt** someone, you stop them in the middle of what they are doing. *Stephen's sister interrupted him while he was listening to music.*

## into

**1** If you go **into** a building, you go inside it.

**2** If something turns **into** something else, it becomes that thing. *Caterpillars turn into butterflies.*

## invent

**invents inventing invented**

If you **invent** something, you make something that nobody has made before.

## invention

**inventions**

An **invention** is something that nobody has made or thought of before. *My uncle's latest invention is a machine that makes his bed.*

## invisible

If something is **invisible**, no one can see it.

# invitation

**invitations**

When you give someone an **invitation**, you ask them to do something with you.

You are invited to:
Lucy's party!
On Sat 1st March, 12.00
At 12 Hazel Grove,
Nutley NT3 4TY

# iron

**irons**

▲ rhymes with **lion**

1 **Iron** is a strong, hard metal. Gates are often made of iron.

2 People use an **iron** to make their clothes smooth. An iron has a handle and a flat metal bottom that gets hot.

# irritable

If someone feels **irritable**, they are cross and easily annoyed. *Sam gets **irritable** when he hasn't had enough sleep.*

# island

**islands**

▲ say **eye**-lund

An **island** is a piece of land with water all around it.

# isn't

**Isn't** is a short way of saying **is not**. *Todd **isn't** coming today.*

# itch

**itches itching itched**

If your skin **itches**, you want to scratch it.

# it's

1 **It's** is a short way of saying **it is**. *It's very cold today.*

2 **It's** is also a short way of saying **it has**. *It's been a long day.*

# its

**Its** means belonging to it. *The cat is playing with its ball.*

# itself

**Itself** means it and nothing else. *This machine works by **itself**.*

# I've

**I've** is a short way of saying **I have**. *I've got an idea for a story.*

# jacket

**jackets**

A **jacket** is a short, light coat.

A B C D E F G H I J K L M N O P Q R S T U V W X Y Z

## jam

**jams**

**Jam** is a sweet food that is made by boiling fruit and sugar together. *Strawberry **jam** on toast.*

## jar

**jars**

**Jars** are containers with lids, usually made of glass. People buy jam and honey in jars.

## jaw

**jaws**

Your **jaw** is the bone at the bottom of your face. It moves when you speak or eat.

## jealous

If you are **jealous**, you are upset because somebody else has something that you do not. *Tom was **jealous** when Charlie got his new computer.*

## jeans

**Jeans** are trousers that are made from a strong cotton material called denim.

## jelly

**jellies**

**Jelly** is a sweet, clear food that wobbles when you move it.

Some words that begin with a "j" sound, such as **generous**, **gentle**, **gerbil** and **giant**, are spelt with a "g".

## jet

**jets**

A **jet** is an aircraft that travels very fast. Jets have special engines.

## jewel

**jewels**

A **jewel** is a very valuable stone. Diamonds are jewels.

## jewellery

**Jewellery** is the name for pretty things, such as necklaces, rings and earrings, that you wear on your body or on your clothes.

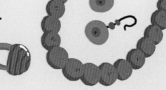

## jigsaw

**jigsaws**

A **jigsaw** is a type of puzzle in which you put lots of pieces back together to make a picture. *Josiah played with his **jigsaw**.*

## job
**jobs**
1 A **job** is the work that someone does to earn money. *Mum has a job in an office.*
2 A **job** is also something that needs to be done. *There are lots of jobs to do in the garden.*

## join
**joins joining joined**
1 If you **join** things, you put them together. *Louise joined the pieces of wood to make a table.*
2 If you **join** a club, you become a member of it. *Heidi has joined a gymnastics club.*

## joint
**joints**
A **joint** is a part of your body where bones meet. Elbows and knees are joints.

## joke
**jokes**
A **joke** is something that you say to make people laugh.

## journey
**journeys**
When you go on a **journey**, you travel from one place to another. *Annabel has a long journey to school.*

## jug
**jugs**
A **jug** is a container with a handle used to hold and pour liquid.

## juggle
**juggles juggling juggled**
When you **juggle**, you keep things in the air by throwing and catching them, one after the other. *Leo can juggle with balls and clubs.*

## juice
**juices**
**Juice** is the liquid that comes from fruit or vegetables. *Zoe loves mango juice.*

## jump
**jumps jumping jumped**
When you **jump**, you bend your knees and push yourself into the air.

*Leah jumped over the puddle.*

Some other words for **jump** are **leap, spring** and **bound.**

## jumper
**jumpers**
A **jumper** is a piece of clothing that covers the top part of your body. Jumpers are often made of wool, and are worn over other clothes.

## jungle
**jungles**
A **jungle** is a place in a hot country where lots of trees and plants grow closely together.

## junk
**Junk** is a name for things people do not want.

## jury
**juries**
A **jury** is a group of people in a court who decide whether someone has broken a law or not.

## just
1 If something has **just** happened, it happened a very short time ago. *Hamish just left.*
2 **Just** also means in every way. *That's just what I mean.*
3 **Just** also means only. *Don't worry about the noise. It's just the wind in the trees.*

## kangaroo
**kangaroos**
A **kangaroo** is a large animal that moves by jumping. Female kangaroos carry their babies in a bag on their stomach called a pouch.

## keen
**keener keenest**
If you are **keen** to do something, you really want to do it.

## keep
**keeps keeping kept**
1 When you **keep** something, you have it and do not give it away. *Alex keeps all his old comics.*
2 If you **keep** doing something, you do it again and again. *Maya kept laughing at me.*
3 If you **keep** doing something, you don't stop doing it. *Keep going, everyone.*
4 **Keep** also means to make something stay the same. *Please keep the door closed.*

## kennel

**kennels**

A **kennel** is a small hut that is made for a dog to sleep in.

## kept

**Kept** comes from the word **keep**. *Connor keeps his diary under his bed. He has always **kept** it there.*

## kettle

**kettles**
You use a **kettle** to boil water. A kettle has a handle and a spout.

*The **kettle** is boiling.*

## key

**keys**
1 A **key** is a piece of metal that has been cut into a special shape. You use a key to open a lock or to start a car.

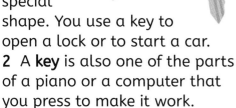

2 A **key** is also one of the parts of a piano or a computer that you press to make it work.

## keyboard

**keyboards**
1 A **keyboard** is the part of a computer with lots of buttons that you use to type letters and numbers.
2 A **keyboard** is also a musical instrument like a piano.

## kick

**kicks kicking kicked**
When you **kick** something, you hit it with your foot. *Rhys **kicked** the football into the air.*

## kid

**kids**
1 A **kid** is a child.
2 A **kid** is also a young goat.

## kill

**kills killing killed**
To **kill** means to make something die. *The frost has **killed** most of the plants.*

## kind

**kinds**
Things of the same **kind** are alike or belong to the same group. *A butterfly is a **kind** of insect.*

## kind

**kinder kindest**
A **kind** person cares about how people feel, and tries to help them. *It was **kind** of Dot to give us tea.*
■ *opposite* **cruel**

a b c d e f g h i j k l m n o p q r s t u v w x y z

**105**

# king

**kings**
A **king** is a man who rules a country. Kings come from royal families and are not chosen by the people.

# kiss

**kisses kissing kissed**
When you **kiss** someone, you touch them with your lips.

# kitchen

**kitchens**
A **kitchen** is a room where you cook meals.

# kite

**kites**
A **kite** is a frame covered with paper or cloth with a very long string attached to it. You can fly a kite in the wind.

# kitten

**kittens**
A **kitten** is a very young cat.

> Words that start with "**kn**" are said with an "**n**" sound.

# knee

**knees**
Your **knee** is the joint in the middle of your leg, where it bends.

# kneel

**kneels kneeling knelt**
When you **kneel**, you get down on your knees.

# knew

**Knew** comes from the word **know**. *Chloe didn't know about the party, but she **knew** that we were planning something.*

# knife

**knives**
A **knife** is a tool that you use to cut things. Knives have a handle and a metal blade.

# knight

**knights**
A **knight** was a type of soldier who lived hundreds of years ago. Knights wore armour and fought for their king.

## knit

**knits knitting knitted**
When you **knit**, you make clothes from wool using two long needles. *Meg is knitting a scarf.*

## knob

**knobs**
A **knob** is a round handle on a door or a drawer.

## knock

**knocks knocking knocked**
1 If you **knock** something, you hit it. *I knocked on the door until someone heard me.*
2 If you **knock** something **over**, you make it fall. *Charlie has knocked over a glass of milk.*

## knot

**knots**
A **knot** is a place where something, such as string, is tied. *Tie a knot to fasten your laces.*

## know

**knows knowing knew known**
1 If you **know** something, you have it in your mind. *Eva knows the answers to all the teacher's questions.*
2 If you **know** someone, you have met them before. *I have known Henry for years.*

# Ll

## label

**labels**
A **label** is a piece of paper or cloth that is attached to something. Clothes often have labels that tell you how to wash them.

## lace

**laces**
**Laces** are like long pieces of string. You use laces to tie your shoes or boots.

## ladder

**ladders**
A **ladder** is a set of steps that can be moved around. *Dad used a ladder to climb up to the roof.*

## lady

**ladies**
**Lady** is a polite word for a woman.

## ladybird

**ladybirds**
A **ladybird** is a small, spotted beetle.

## laid

**Laid** comes from the word **lay**. *I asked Mason to lay the clothes on the chair, but he laid them on the bed.*

A
B
C
D
E
F
G
H
I
J
K
L
M
N
O
P
Q
R
S
T
U
V
W
X
Y
Z

## lake

**lakes**
A **lake** is a large area of water with land all around it.

## lamb

**lambs**
1  A **lamb** is a young sheep.
2  **Lamb** is also the meat that comes from lambs.

## lamp

**lamps**
A **lamp** makes light. Most lamps work by electricity. *Jenny has a lamp by her bed.*

## land

**Land** is the name for the parts of the Earth that are not covered by water.

## land

**lands landing landed**
When a plane **lands**, it comes down from the air to the ground.

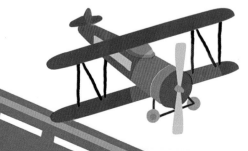

## landing

**landings**
A **landing** is the area of a house at the top of the stairs. A landing has other rooms coming off it.

## lane

**lanes**
1  A **lane** is a narrow road, usually in the country.
2  A **lane** is also one of the strips that a wide road is divided into.

## language

**languages**
**Language** is a name for the set of words people use to speak and write to each other. *Fritz can speak three languages.*

## lantern

**lanterns**
A **lantern** is a lamp that you carry. Lanterns sometimes have a candle inside them.

## lap

**laps**
Your **lap** is the top part of your legs when you are sitting down. *The kitten sat on Daisy's lap.*

## lap

**laps lapping lapped**
When an animal **laps up** a drink, it uses its tongue to drink it.

# laptop
**laptops**
A **laptop** is a small computer that you can carry around with you.

# large
**larger largest**
If something is **large**, it takes up a lot of space. *A **large** room. A **large** bag of sweets.*

# last
**lasts lasting lasted**
If something **lasts**, it carries on happening. *The party **lasted** for three hours.*

# last
1 Something that is **last** comes at the end. *Z is the **last** letter of the alphabet.*
■ opposite **first**
2 **Last** also means the one before this. *I saw Liam **last** week.*
■ opposite **next**

# late
**later latest**
1 If you are **late**, you arrive after the right time. *Tom was **late** because his watch was wrong.*
2 **Late** also means near the end of something. *We arrived home **late** in the evening.*
■ opposite **early**
3 **Latest** also means most recent. *Have you heard his **latest** song?*

# laugh
**laughs laughing laughed**
▲ *rhymes with* **staff**
When you **laugh**, you make sounds that show that you think that something is funny. *Laura always **laughs** at Mike's jokes.*

# law
**laws**
A **law** is a rule that everyone in a country must obey.

# lawn
**lawns**
A **lawn** is an area of grass that is kept short. Parks and gardens have lawns.

# lay
**lays laying laid**
1 If you **lay** something somewhere, you put it down carefully.
2 If you **lay a table**, you get it ready for a meal. *Tony **laid the table** for dinner.*
3 When a bird **lays** an egg, the egg comes out of its body. *Our hen has **laid** an egg.*

# lay
**Lay** comes from the word **lie**. *Sienna decided to lie on the sofa. She **lay** there for hours.*

## layer

**layers**

A **layer** is something flat that lies on top of, or beneath, something else.

*My birthday cake has three layers.*

## lazy

**lazier laziest**

Someone who is **lazy** does not want to do any work. *Jack is too lazy to do his homework.*

## lead

**leads**

1  A **lead** is a long strip of leather or a chain that you fix to a dog's collar. You hold the end of the lead and use it to control the dog.

▲ *rhymes with* **seed**

2  The **lead** in a pencil is the black part that makes a mark.

▲ *rhymes with* **head**

## lead

**leads leading led**

▲ *rhymes with* **seed**

1  If you **lead** someone to a place, you go in front of them to show them where it is.

2  If you **lead** a group of people, you are in charge of them.

## leaf

**leaves**

A **leaf** is one of the thin, flat parts of a plant or a tree. Leaves are usually green but many change colour in autumn.

## leak

**leaks leaking leaked**

If a container **leaks**, the liquid inside it comes out slowly through a small hole when you don't want it to.

## lean

**leans leaning leant**

If something **leans**, it bends to one side. *The tower leant to one side.*

## learn

**learns learning learnt**

When you **learn** something, you get to know it or understand it. *Emma is learning to play tennis.*

## least

**Least** means the smallest amount. *Nobody ate much, but Amelia ate least.*

■ *opposite* **most**

## leather

**Leather** is made from animal skin. It is used to make shoes and bags.

leather bag

## leave

**leaves leaving left**
**1** If you **leave** a place, you go away from it. *I **left** home early this morning.*
**2** When you **leave** something in a place, you let it stay where it is. *I **left** my jacket at home.*

## led

**Led** comes from the word **lead**. *Chris will lead us up the mountain. He has **led** us before.*

## leek

**leeks**
A **leek** is a long, white vegetable with green leaves at one end.

## left

You have a **left** hand and a right hand. Most people write with their right hand, but some people use their left hand.
■ *opposite* **right**

## left

**Left** comes from the word **leave**. *We promised to leave before it got dark, so we **left** at about five o'clock.*

## leg

**legs**
**1** Your **legs** are the parts of your body that you use for standing and walking.
**2** The **legs** on a table or a chair are the parts that hold it up.

## lemon

**lemons**
A **lemon** is a yellow fruit with a thick skin. Lemons are juicy and have a sharp taste.

## lend

**lends lending lent**
If you **lend** something to someone, you let them have it for a short time. *I **lent** Craig my pen.*

## length

**lengths**
The **length** of something is how long it is. *Dad measured the **length** of the wood.*

## lens

**lenses**
A **lens** is a special, curved piece of glass or plastic. Lenses are used in glasses and telescopes to make things look clearer or bigger.

## lent

**Lent** comes from the word **lend**. *Robby often lends me his bicycle. He **lent** it to me yesterday.*

# leopard

**leopards**

▲ *say lep-erd*

A **leopard** is a large wild cat. Leopards have dark yellow fur with black spots.

# leotard

**leotards**

▲ *say lee-oh-tard*

A **leotard** is a piece of clothing that fits tightly. You may wear a leotard when you dance or do exercise. *Laura wears a **leotard** for her ballet class.*

# less

**Less** means not as much. *I had **less** to eat than my brother.*

■ *opposite* **more**

# lesson

**lessons**

A **lesson** is a period of time when you are taught something. *A swimming **lesson**.*

# let

**lets letting let**

If someone **lets** you do something, they say that you can do it. *Dad **let** us stay up late.*

# let's

**Let's** is a short way of saying **let us**. *Let's go to the cinema.*

# letter

**letters**

1 A **letter** is a sign that you use to write words. A, m and z are letters.

2 A **letter** is also a message that you write on paper. You usually put letters in envelopes to post them.

23 Duck St
Puddletown
Dorset
DT2 3SH
2oth March

Dear Gran,
    Thank you so much for the art set you sent for my birthday. I've painted a picture of you. I hope you like it!

Lots of love,
        Meg xXx

# lettuce

**lettuces**

▲ *say let-iss*

A **lettuce** is a vegetable with large leaves that are usually green. You use lettuce to make salads.

## level
**levels**
In computer games, **levels** measure your progress, and usually get more difficult as you go on. *I've got to level four already.*

## level
Something that is **level** is flat and not sloping. *Football pitches should be level.*

## library
**libraries**
A **library** is a place where a lot of books are kept. You can borrow books from a library to read at home.

## lick
**licks licking licked**
If you **lick** something, you move your tongue along it.

*Leila licked her lolly.*

## lid
**lids**
A **lid** is the top of a box or other container. To open the container, you lift up the lid or take it off.

## lie
**lies lying lied**
If you **lie**, you say something that is not true.

## lie
**lies lying lay lain**
When you **lie** down, you rest with your body flat on a bed or another surface.

## life
**lives**
**Life** is the time that someone is alive. *My grandfather had a long and interesting life.*

## lift
**lifts**
A **lift** is a little room that goes up and down. Lifts carry people between the floors of a building.

## lift
**lifts lifting lifted**
If you **lift** something, you pick it up. *Jonathan lifted the kitten out of the basket.*

## light
**lights**
1 When there is **light**, you can see things. The Sun, lamps and torches make light.
2 A **light** is something that gives out light, such as a lamp.

A B C D E F G H I J K **L** M N O P Q R S T U V W X Y Z

## light

**lights lighting lit**
When you **light** a fire, you make it burn. *Mum **lit** the bonfire.*

## light

**lighter lightest**
1 If it is **light**, you can see things.
■ *opposite* **dark**
2 **Light** colours are pale.
■ *opposite* **dark**
3 Something that is **light** does not weigh very much.
■ *opposite* **heavy**

## lighthouse

**lighthouses**
A **lighthouse** is a tower with a flashing light on top. Lighthouses warn ships of dangers, such as hidden rocks.

## lightning

**Lightning** is a sudden flash of light in the sky. You sometimes see lightning when there is a storm.

## like

**likes liking liked**
When you **like** something, it pleases you.
■ *opposite* **dislike**

## like

1 If two people are **like** each other, they are the same in some way.
2 **Like** also means such as. *Will enjoys hobbies **like** dancing and cycling.*

## line

**lines**
1 A **line** is a long, thin mark. *My writing paper has **lines** printed on it.*
2 A **line** is also a number of people or things in a row. *We stood in a **line** for the team photograph.*

## link

**links**
A **link** is a word or a picture on a web page that you can click on to go to another web page or website.

## lion

**lions**
A **lion** is a large wild cat with light brown fur. Lions live in Africa and India.

# lip

**lips**
Your **lips** are the edges of your mouth.

# liquid

**liquids**
A **liquid** is something that can be poured. Water, oil and fruit juice are all liquids.

# list

**lists**
A **list** is a group of things that are written down one after the other. *A shopping list.*

# listen

**listens listening listened**
When you **listen**, you pay attention to what you are hearing. *Mrs Parsnip asked everybody to **listen** carefully.*

# lit

**Lit** comes from the word **light**. *Dad decided to light a fire. He **lit** it a long way from the house.*

# litter

1 **Litter** is rubbish that has been dropped outside. *The streets were dirty and full of **litter**.*
2 A **litter** is a group of baby animals born at the same time to the same mother. *A **litter** of puppies.*

# little

1 If something is **little**, it is small.
2 **Little** also means not much. *Martin eats very **little**.*

# live

**lives living lived**
▲ *rhymes with* **give**
1 Something that **lives** is alive.
2 If you **live** somewhere, your home is there. *Mohammed **lives** in London.*

# live

▲ *rhymes with* **hive**
**Live** means happening at the same time as you watch it. *This show comes to you **live** from New York City.*

# lively

**livelier liveliest**
Someone who is **lively** has a lot of energy.
*Laura is a **lively** dancer.*

# lizard

**lizards**
A **lizard** is a reptile with a long body and a tail. Lizards lay eggs.

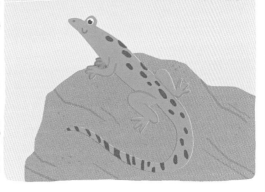

a b c d e f g h i j k **l** m n o p q r s t u v w x y z

## load
**loads**
A **load** is something heavy that has to be moved. *The truck took a **load** of sand to the house.*

## loaf
**loaves**
A **loaf** is bread that has been baked in a shape.

## lobster
**lobsters**
A **lobster** is a sea creature with a shell and ten legs. You can eat lobsters. Lobsters turn pink when you cook them.

claw or pincer

feeler

## lock
**locks**
A **lock** keeps things such as doors and cupboards shut. You need a key to open a lock. *My diary has a **lock** on it.*

## log
**logs**
A **log** is a thick piece of wood that has been cut from a tree.

## lolly
**lollies**
A **lolly** is a sweet or ice cream on a stick.

## lonely
**lonelier loneliest**
If you are **lonely**, you feel unhappy because you are alone.

## long
**longer longest**
**1** If something is **long**, its ends are far away from each other. *Kamala has very **long** hair.*
**2** If something takes a **long** time, it takes a lot of time.
■ *opposite* **short**

## look
**looks looking looked**
**1** When you **look** at something, you use your eyes to see it. *Jemima is **looking** at the view.*
**2** How something **looks** is how it seems. *That new game **looks** amazing.*
**3** If you **look for** something, you try to find it.

## loop
**loops**
A **loop** is a circle made with a rope, a string or a ribbon.

loop

*A bow has two **loops**.*

## loose
**looser loosest**
▲ *rhymes with* **goose**
1 Clothes that are **loose** do not fit closely. ***Loose** trousers.*
2 Something that is **loose** is not fixed firmly. *A **loose** handle.*
■ *opposite* **tight**

## lorry
**lorries**
A **lorry** is a large vehicle used for carrying things.

## lose
**loses losing lost**
▲ *rhymes with* **shoes**
1 If you **lose** a game or a race, you do not win it.
■ *opposite* **win**
2 If you **lose** something, you do not know where it is. *Justin has **lost** his watch.*
■ *opposite* **find**

## lost
If you are **lost**, you do not know where you are, or which way to go.

## lot
**lots**
A **lot** is a large amount. *I had a **lot** of birthday cards. **Lots** of people came to my party.*

## loud
**louder loudest**
Something that is **loud** makes a lot of noise. *Mum hates **loud** music.*
■ *opposite* **quiet**

## lounge
**lounges**
A **lounge** is a room where you can sit and relax.

## love
**loves loving loved**
If you **love** someone, you like them very much.

## lovely
**lovelier loveliest**
If you think something is **lovely**, it really pleases you. *A **lovely** view. A **lovely** song.*

## low
**lower lowest**
1 Something that is **low** is not far from the ground.
2 **Low** also means smaller than usual. *A **low** chair.*
*Low prices. A **low** temperature.*
3 A **low** voice goes down a long way. Most men have low voices.
■ *opposite* **high**

## lucky

**luckier luckiest**
If you are **lucky**, good things happen to you that you have not planned.

## luggage

**Luggage** is the name for the cases and bags that you take with you when you travel.

## lump

**lumps**
1  A **lump** is a piece of something. *A lump of pastry. A lump of coal.*
2  A **lump** is something round that sticks out. *My sauce has lumps in it. Look at this lump on my head!*

## lunch

**lunches**
**Lunch** is the meal that you eat in the middle of the day. *Florence always takes a packed lunch to school.*

## lung

**lungs**
Your **lungs** are inside your chest. When you breathe, air goes in and out of your lungs.

## lying

**Lying** comes from the word **lie**. *Mum told me never to lie. She was very angry when she heard me lying to Jack.*

# Mm

## machine

**machines**
A **machine** is something that does a job. Machines have many moving parts. Cars, computers and cranes are all machines.

## made

**Made** comes from the word **make**. *Freya makes excellent cakes. Yesterday, she made a fruitcake.*

## magic

1  In stories, **magic** is the power to make impossible things happen.
2  **Magic** is also a name for clever tricks that look impossible.

*He worked his magic and a rabbit came out of the hat!*

## magician

**magicians**
A **magician** is someone who does surprising tricks. *Dan had a magician at his party.*

## magnet

**magnets**
A **magnet** is a special piece of metal that makes other metals stick to it. Things that are made of iron and steel stick to magnets.

## magnifying glass

**magnifying glasses**
A **magnifying glass** is a glass lens that makes things look bigger.

## mail

**Mail** is a name for the letters and parcels that people post.

## main

**Main** means the biggest or the most important. *The main entrance to the station. The main meal of the day.*

## make

**makes making made**
1 If you **make** something, you put it together. *Evan loves making model planes.*
2 If you **make** something happen, it happens because of what you do. *Sophia teased her sister and made her cry.*
3 If you **make** something **up**, you invent it. *Alice is always making up stories.*
4 If you **make up** with someone, you become friends again after a quarrel.

## make-up

**Make-up** is something such as lipstick that people put on their face or body to change how they look.

## male

A **male** person or animal belongs to the sex that cannot have babies.

## mammal

**mammals**
A **mammal** is an animal that has babies and can feed them with its own milk. Human beings, dogs and whales are all mammals.

## man

**men**
A **man** is an adult, male human being.

## manage

**manages managing managed**

If you **manage** to do something, you do it even though it is difficult. *Poppy managed to swim 20 lengths of the pool.*

## manners

Your **manners** are the way that you behave. *Gregory has very good manners. He is always polite and helpful.*

## many

**Many** means a large number. *There are many flowers in our garden.*

## map

**maps**

A **map** is a drawing that shows you where places are. Maps can show roads, rivers and buildings.

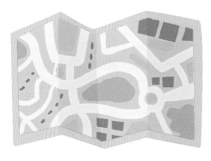

## marble

**marbles**

**1** A **marble** is a small, glass ball that is used to play a game called marbles.
**2** **Marble** is a hard rock. Statues and buildings can be made from marble.

## march

**marches marching marched**

When soldiers **march**, they all walk together with steps of the same size.

## margarine

▲ *say marj-er-**een***

**Margarine** is a soft, yellow food like butter. You can spread margarine on bread or use it for cooking.

## margin

**margins**

A **margin** is a long, blank space along the edge of a page.

## mark

**marks**

**1** A **mark** is a dirty spot or a stain on something.
**2** Teachers give you a **mark** to show how good or bad your work is.

## market

**markets**

A **market** is a place where you can buy things. Markets are often held outdoors.

## marmalade

**Marmalade** is a sweet, sticky food made from oranges or lemons. People eat marmalade on toast for breakfast.

## marry

**marries marrying married**
When two people **marry**, they promise to spend their lives together.

## marsh

**marshes**
A **marsh** is an area of wet and muddy land. Many birds and animals live in marshes.

## mask

**masks**
A **mask** is something you wear to cover your face.

## mat

**mats**
1 A **mat** is a small piece of carpet or other material that is used to cover part of a floor.
2 A **mat** is also a small piece of cloth or other material that you put on a table to protect it.

## match

**matches**
1 A **match** is a short, thin stick of wood with a special tip. It produces a flame when you rub its tip on a strip on the side of the matchbox.
2 A **match** is a game played by two players or two teams. *A football **match**.*

## match

**matches matching matched**
If two or more things **match**, they look the same in some way. *Jessica's hat, scarf and gloves all match.*

## material

**materials**
1 **Material** is a name for anything used to make something else. Bricks, wood and glass are all building materials.
2 **Material** is also a name for wool, cotton and other kinds of cloth. *Sienna's dress is made from thick **material**.*

## maths

When you study **maths**, you learn about numbers, amounts and shapes.

## matter

**matters mattering mattered**
If something **matters** to you, you care a lot about it and think that it is important. *It **matters** to me that you come to my party.*

## mattress

**mattresses**
A **mattress** is the thick, soft part of a bed that you lie on. Mattresses often have springs inside them.

## may

**might**
1 If something **may** happen, there is a chance that it will happen. *Susie **may** come round today.*
*See also **might***
2 If you **may** do something, you are allowed to do it. *Please **may** I use the computer?*

## meadow

**meadows**
A **meadow** is a field of grass.

## meal

**meals**
A **meal** is the food you eat at certain times of the day. Breakfast, lunch and dinner are meals.

## mean

**means meaning meant**
1 When you say what something **means**, you explain it. *William told us what the signs **meant**.*
2 If you **mean** to do something, you plan to do it. *I didn't **mean** to hurt my brother.*

## mean

**meaner meanest**
Someone who is **mean** is not generous or kind.

## measure

**measures measuring measured**
When you **measure** something, you find out how big it is.

## meat

**Meat** is a kind of food that comes from animals. Beef, lamb and chicken are types of meat.

## medal

**medals**
**Medals** are given to people as prizes or rewards. They often look like a coin hanging from a ribbon.

# medicine
**medicines**
▲ *say med-ih-suhn*
Medicine is something that sick people take to make them better.

# medium
Medium means between large and small in size.

# meet
**meets meeting met**
When you **meet** someone, you both go to the same place and you see each other. *I met Lucy outside the museum.*

# melt
**melts melting melted**
When something **melts**, it gets warmer and turns into a liquid. *My snowman melted in the sunshine.*

# member
**members**
If you are a **member** of a group, you are one of the people in it.

# memory
You use your **memory** to remember things. If you have a good memory, you remember things. If you have a bad memory, you forget them.

# mend
**mends mending mended**
If you **mend** something that is broken, you put it right so that it can be used again.

*Dylan is mending his kite.*

# menu
**menus**
A **menu** is a list of food that you can buy in a restaurant or a café.

# mermaid
**mermaids**
In stories, **mermaids** are magical creatures that look like beautiful women with fish tails instead of legs.

# mess
If something is a **mess**, it is very untidy and sometimes dirty. *Your bedroom is a mess!*

## message

**messages**
A **message** is a piece of information that you send to someone or leave for someone.

*Don't forget your lunch!*

## met

**Met** comes from the word **meet**. *Our club meets every week. Last term, it met on Fridays.*

## metal

**metals**
A **metal** is a hard material that is found in the ground. Metals are used to make things such as machines, vehicles and jewellery. Iron and gold are metals.

## microphone

**microphones**
You use a **microphone** to make your voice sound louder.

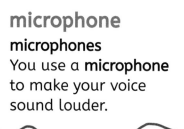

## microscope

**microscopes**
A **microscope** makes small things look much bigger, so that you can see and study them. *We looked at leaves and petals through a microscope.*

## midday

**Midday** is 12 o'clock in the middle of the day.

## middle

**middles**
1 The **middle** of something is the place that is the same distance away from all of its sides. *There's a tree in the middle of our garden.*
2 If you are **in the middle of** something, you have started it but aren't close to finishing it yet. *Alice is in the middle of watching her favourite programme.*

## midnight

**Midnight** is 12 o'clock in the middle of the night.

## might

**Might** comes from the word **may**. *We may go out today. Sarah said she might come too.*

## milk

**Milk** is a white liquid that mothers feed to their babies. People often drink cows' milk.

## mime

**mimes miming mimed**
When you **mime**, you act without using any words. *Ella mimed being trapped in a big box.*

## mind

**minds**
Your **mind** is the part of you that thinks, remembers and imagines.

## mind

**minds minding minded**
If you **mind** something, it bothers you. *Do you mind if I turn up the TV?*

## mine

**mines**
A **mine** is a place where things, such as coal or diamonds, are dug out of the ground.

## mine

If something belongs to me, then it is **mine**. *Don't touch that chocolate. It's mine!*

## minus

**Minus** means take away. The sign for minus is **–**. *Ten minus four is six.*

$$10-4=6$$

■ *opposite* **plus**

## minute

**minutes**
▲ *say min-it*
A **minute** is an amount of time. There are 60 seconds in a minute, and 60 minutes in an hour.

## mirror

**mirrors**
A **mirror** is a special piece of glass that you can see yourself in. *Nat is looking at himself in the mirror.*

## mischievous

▲ *say miss-chiv-us*
Someone who is **mischievous** is lively and naughty. *The mischievous children helped themselves to the cake.*

## miserable

Someone who is **miserable** feels sad and unhappy. *Robin is miserable because it is raining.*

## miss

**misses missing missed**
1 If you **miss** someone, you are unhappy because they are not with you.
2 If you **miss** a train or a bus, you do not manage to catch it.
3 If you **miss** a target, you do not manage to hit it.

## missing

If something is **missing**, it isn't where it should be.

a b c d e f g h i j k l m n o p q r s t u v w x y z

## mist

**Mist** is a cloud that is close to the ground. When there is a mist, you cannot see very far.

## mistake

**mistakes**
If you make a **mistake**, you do or say something that is wrong.

## mix

**mixes mixing mixed**
1 When you **mix** things, you put them together to make one thing. *Joe **mixed** red and yellow paint to make orange paint.*
2 If you **mix** things **up**, you get them the wrong way round.

## mixture

**mixtures**
A **mixture** is something you make by mixing things together. *Mud is a **mixture** of earth and water.*

## moan

**moans moaning moaned**
1 If you **moan**, you make a long, low sound because you are unhappy or hurt.
2 If you **moan** about something, you say that you are unhappy about it. *Robin was **moaning** because it was too wet to go outside.*

## mobile phone

**mobile phones**
A **mobile phone** is a small telephone that you can carry around with you.

## model

**models**
A **model** is a small copy of something. *Jake has a **model** of a sailing boat inside a bottle.*

## mole

**moles**
A **mole** is a small animal with strong front claws that lives under the ground.

## moment

**moments**
A **moment** is a very short amount of time. *Wait a **moment** while I shut the door.*

## money

**Money** is the name for the coins and notes that you use to buy things.

## monkey

**monkeys**
A **monkey** is an animal with long arms and legs, a very long tail and a furry body. Monkeys live in trees in hot countries.

## monster

**monsters**
In stories, a **monster** is a strange and horrible creature that is very dangerous. Monsters are often very large, like dragons.

## month

**months**
1  There are twelve **months** in a year. May and July are months.
2  A **month** is also any period of about four weeks.

## mood

**moods**
Your **mood** is the way that you feel. *Matilda is in a good mood because she is on holiday.*

## Moon

The **Moon** is the big, bright ball of rock you often see in the sky at night. It takes a month to go round the Earth.

## more

**More** means larger in size or number. *My brother ate more lunch than I did.*
■ opposite **less** or **fewer**

## morning

**mornings**
The **morning** is the part of the day before midday.

## most

**Most** means the largest amount. *My brother ate more than I did, but my father ate **most** of all.*
■ opposite **least** or **fewest**

## moth

**moths**
A **moth** is an insect with four large wings. Moths usually come out at night.

## mother

**mothers**
A **mother** is a woman who has a child.

## motorbike

**motorbikes**
A **motorbike** is a large, heavy bicycle with an engine.

## motorway

**motorways**
A **motorway** is a wide road where vehicles travel fast. People drive long distances on motorways.

## mountain

**mountains**
A **mountain** is a very high piece of land. Mountains are higher than hills.

## mouse

**mice**
1 A **mouse** is a small, furry animal with a long tail and sharp teeth. *The mouse climbed up the wheat stalk.*
2 A **mouse** is also something that you use to move things on a computer screen.

## mouth

**mouths**
Your **mouth** is the part of your face that you use to eat and talk.

## move

**moves moving moved**
▲ *say moov*
1 When things **move**, they change position and do not stay still. *The leaves moved in the breeze.*
2 When people **move**, they go from one place to another. *Andy moved to a more comfortable chair.*
3 **Move** also means to stop living in one place and start living somewhere else. *Amy moved to Wales.*

## movie

**movies**
▲ *say moo-vee*
A **movie** is a film.

## much

**Much** means a large amount. *Tilly doesn't eat much.*

## mud

**Mud** is earth that is wet and sticky.

## mug

**mugs**
A **mug** is a large cup with tall, straight sides.

## multiply

**multiplies multiplying multiplied**
When you **multiply** numbers, you add the same number to itself several times. *Four multiplied by three is twelve.*

$$4 \times 3 = 12$$

■ *opposite* **divide**

## mum

**mums**
**Mum** is a name for your mother.

## muscle

**muscles**
A **muscle** is a part of your body. Muscles are fixed to bones and pull on them to make them move.

## museum

**museums**

A **museum** is a place where you can see a collection of interesting things.

## mushroom

**mushrooms**

A **mushroom** is a plant-like thing with a rounded top on a stalk. You can eat some mushrooms.

## music

**Music** is a pattern of sounds. People make music by playing musical instruments or by singing.

## musical instrument

**musical instruments**

A **musical instrument** is something that you use to make music. You can play musical instruments by blowing into them or hitting them, or by pulling their strings.

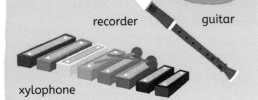

recorder    guitar

xylophone

## must

If you **must** do something, you have to do it. *I must go now.*

## mustn't

**Mustn't** is a short way of saying **must not**. *You mustn't forget to take your umbrella.*

## myself

**Myself** means me and nobody else. *I have hurt myself.*

## mysterious

▲ *say mist-ear-ee-us*

Something that is **mysterious** is difficult to understand or explain. *We heard a mysterious sound.*

# Nn

## nag

**nags nagging nagged**

If someone **nags** you, they keep telling you to do something. *Mum keeps nagging me to do up my laces.*

## nail

**nails**

1 A **nail** is a piece of metal with a point at one end. You use nails to join pieces of wood together.
2 Your **nails** are the hard parts at the ends of your fingers and toes.

## naked

▲ *say nay-kid*

Someone who is **naked** is not wearing any clothes.

m
n

## name

**names**
A **name** is what you call a person or a thing. *My friend's* **name** *is Angus.*

## nap

**naps**
If you have a **nap**, you sleep for a short time.

## napkin

**napkins**
A **napkin** is a piece of cloth or paper that you use to protect your clothes when you eat.

## nappy

**nappies**
A **nappy** is a pad of cloth or tissue that covers a baby's bottom.

## narrow

**narrower narrowest**
If something is **narrow**, its sides are not far apart. *A* **narrow** *path wound between the hills.*
■ opposite **wide**

## nasty

**nastier nastiest**
Someone who is **nasty** is cruel and unkind. *A* **nasty** *witch.*

## natural

Something that is **natural** has not been made by people or machines. Wood is a natural material.

## nature

**Nature** is everything in the world that has not been made by people. Plants, animals and the weather are all parts of nature.

## naughty

**naughtier naughtiest**
Someone who is **naughty** behaves badly. *Sophie was very* **naughty** *today. She threw her lunch out of the window.*

## near

**nearer nearest**
If something is **near**, it is only a short distance away. *The park is very* **near** *our house.*
■ opposite **far**

## nearly

**Nearly** means almost, but not quite. *Ruth is* **nearly** *140 centimetres high. I* **nearly** *won the race today.*

## neat

**neater neatest**
Something that is **neat** is very tidy. *Please make your handwriting* **neat** *so I can read it. Chloe has tidied her bedroom so that it looks really* **neat**.

# neck

**necks**

Your **neck** is the part of your body that joins your head to your shoulders.

# necklace

**necklaces**

A **necklace** is a string of beads or a chain that you wear round your neck.

necklace

Some words that begin with an "**n**" sound, such as **knee, knife, knock** and **know**, are spelt "**kn**".

# need

**needs needing needed**

If you **need** something, you must have it. *Human beings need food and water to live.*

# needle

**needles**

**1** A **needle** is a very thin, pointed piece of metal used for sewing. You put thread through a hole in the needle.

**2 Knitting needles** are long sticks made of plastic or metal. People use knitting needles to knit clothes out of wool.

# neighbour

**neighbours**

A **neighbour** is someone who lives near you.

# neither

**Neither** means not one or the other. *Neither of the boys knew the way home.*

# nephew

**nephews**

Someone's **nephew** is the son of their brother or sister.

# nervous

**1** If you are **nervous** about something, you are worried or excited about it. *Tom is nervous about his first trip on a plane.*

**2** A **nervous** person or animal is easily frightened. *Don't scare the kittens. They're very nervous.*

n

# nest

**nests**

A **nest** is a home made by birds and some animals. Birds keep their eggs and babies in a nest.

nest

131

A B C D E F G H I J K L M **N** O P Q R S T U V W X Y Z

## net

**nets**

1  A **net** is a bag made of knotted thread or rope. Nets are used to catch fish. *Jon caught some fish in his net and then put them back in the water.*
2  When you play tennis, you hit the ball over a **net**. Tennis nets are made of knotted rope.
3  The **net** is a short way of saying the **internet**.

## never

**Never** means not at any time. *I've never climbed a mountain.*
■ opposite **always**

## new

**newer newest**

1  If something is **new**, it has just been made or it has just been bought. *Ruby has a new bicycle.*
2  **New** can also mean different. *There is a new family next door.*
■ opposite **old**

## news

1  **News** is information about things that are happening in the world. *Dad always listens to the news on the radio.*
2  **News** is also information about things that have happened to you. *I've had some good news. I'm in the school team.*

## newspaper

**newspapers**

A **newspaper** is made of several sheets of paper with stories and pictures about the news. Most newspapers come out every day.

## newt

**newts**

A **newt** is a small creature with short legs and a long tail. Newts live on land and lay their eggs in water.

## next

1  **Next** means the one after this. *We're all going on holiday next week.*
■ opposite **last**
2  **Next to** means nearest. *Jason sits next to me at school.*

## nice

**nicer nicest**

If you think that something is **nice**, you like it. *A nice meal. A nice day.*

Some other words for **nice** are **beautiful, pleasant, good, lovely** and **enjoyable**.

## nickname

**nicknames**

A **nickname** is a name that you give to a friend. *Finn's nickname is Fish because he swims so well.*

# niece

**nieces**

Someone's **niece** is the daughter of their brother or sister.

# night

**Night** is the time when it is dark outside. People sleep at night.

■ *opposite* **day**

# nightie

**nighties**

A **nightie** is a loose dress that girls and women wear in bed.

*Rowena has a purple nightie.*

# nightmare

**nightmares**

A **nightmare** is a horrible, frightening dream.

# nobody

**Nobody** means no person. *There was nobody in the house.*

# nod

**nods nodding nodded**

When you **nod**, you move your head up and down. People often nod to show that they agree.

# noise

**noises**

A **noise** is a sound. *We heard a noise coming from the cellar.*

# noisy

**noisier noisiest**

If something is **noisy**, it is very loud. *I wish that Rupert's drums were not quite so noisy.*

# none

**None** means not one or not any. *Jonathan went to buy some doughnuts, but there were none left.*

# nonsense

Something that is **nonsense** is silly and does not mean anything. *Katy is talking nonsense again.*

# noon

**Noon** is 12 o'clock in the middle of the day.

# no one

**No one** means no person. *There was no one in when I got home.*

# normal

Something that is **normal** is ordinary and usual. *I got up at the normal time.*

# north

**North** is a direction. If you face the Sun when it rises, north is on your left.
■ *opposite* **south**

# nose

**noses**
Your **nose** is the part of your face that you use to smell and breathe.

# note

**notes**
1 A **note** is a sound that you make when you sing or play a musical instrument.
2 A **note** is also a sign that stands for a musical note.
3 A **note** is also a short message that you write down.
4 A **note** is also a piece of paper money. *A £5 note.*

# nothing

**Nothing** means not a thing. *There was **nothing** left in Pepper's bowl.*

# notice

**notices noticing noticed**
If you **notice** something, you see it and pay attention to it. *Melina **noticed** that Fiona looked pale.*

# now

**Now** means at this time. *It's raining **now**, so let's go out later.*

# nowhere

**Nowhere** means no place. *There was **nowhere** we could hide.*

# number

**numbers**
A **number** is a word or a sign that shows you how many there are. Four and thirty-three are numbers. 9 and 27 are also numbers.

# nurse

**nurses**
A **nurse** is someone who looks after people who are ill or hurt. Nurses often work in hospitals.

# nursery

**nurseries**
A **nursery** is a place where young children are looked after while their parents are at work.

# nut

**nuts**
A **nut** is a seed with a hard shell. Many nuts can be eaten.

cashews

walnuts

hazelnuts

# Oo

## oar

**oars**
An **oar** is a long pole with a wide end. You use oars to row a boat.

## obey

**obeys obeying obeyed**
When you **obey** someone, you do what they tell you. *Connor is teaching his puppy to **obey** him.*
■ *opposite* **disobey**

## object

**objects**
An **object** is a thing that you can touch and see. Objects are not alive. Computers, toys, books and furniture are all objects.

## obvious

If something is **obvious**, it is easy to see or easy to understand.

## ocean

**oceans**
An **ocean** is a very large sea. There are five oceans in the world.

## o'clock

You use the word **o'clock** when you say what time it is. O'clock is short for of the clock. *It is now seven **o'clock**.*

## octopus

**octopuses**
An **octopus** is a sea creature with a soft body and eight long legs.

## odd

**odder oddest**
1  An **odd** number cannot be divided exactly by two. 1, 3, 5 and 7 are odd numbers.
■ *opposite* **even**
2  If something is **odd**, it is strange or unusual. *Oscar has the **odd** habit of scratching his knees when he's nervous.*
3  **Odd** things are not part of a pair or a set. *Ben was wearing **odd** socks.*

## off

1  **Off** means away from something. *Take the plates **off** the table.*
2  When you turn a machine **off**, you make it stop working.
■ *opposite* **on**

a b c d e f g h i j k l m n o p q r s t u v w x y z

## offer

**offers offering offered**

1 If you **offer** to do something, you say that you will do it without being asked. *Adam offered to make the tea.*

2 If you **offer** someone something, you ask them if they would like it. *Tilly offered a sandwich to her aunt.*

## office

**offices**

An **office** is a room or a building where people work at desks.

## often

If you do something **often**, you do it a lot. *We often go skating.*

## oil

**oils**

Oil is a thick liquid. Some oil comes from the ground and is used to help machines run, or to make heat. Some oil comes from plants and is used for cooking.

## old

**older oldest**

1 Someone who is **old** has lived for a long time. *An old man.*

■ *opposite* **young**

2 Something that is **old** has been used for a long time. *Old clothes.*

■ *opposite* **new**

## on

1 **On** means touching the surface of something. *Put the plates on the table.*

2 When you turn a machine **on** you make it start working.

■ *opposite* **off**

3 **On** also means about. *Louise bought a book on cats.*

4 You use **on** to say when something happens. *We went out for lunch on Friday.*

## once

▲ *say* **wunce**

1 If something happens **once**, it happens one time. *I've only been to London once.*

2 **Once** also means after. *Once we've had lunch, we can go out.*

## onion

**onions**

An **onion** is a round vegetable with a strong taste and smell. Onions grow under the ground.

## online

**Online** means on the internet. *I read about it online.*

## only

▲ *say* **own-lee**

**Only** means just that and not any more. *There's only one cake left.*

# onto

To move **onto** something is to get on it, or on top of it. *Get onto the bus. He threw his coat onto the chair.*

# open

**opens opening opened**
1 If you **open** a door, you move it so that you can go through it.
2 If you **open** a box, you take its lid off, so that you can put things in or take things out of it.
■ *opposite* **close**

# open

If something is **open**, people can go through it or into it. *The door is open. The shop is open all day.*
■ *opposite* **closed**

# operation

**operations**
When someone has an **operation**, part of their body is repaired, replaced or removed.

# opposite

**opposites**
The **opposite** of something is the thing that is most different from it. *The opposite of day is night.*

day
night

# opposite

If two people are **opposite** one another, they face each other. *My friend sat opposite me, on the other side of the table.*

# orange

**oranges**
1 **Orange** is the colour that you make when you mix red and yellow. Carrots are orange.
2 An **orange** is a round, juicy fruit with a thick, orange skin.

# orchard

**orchards**
An **orchard** is a piece of land where fruit trees are grown.

# orchestra

**orchestras**
An **orchestra** is a large group of people who play different musical instruments together. *The orchestra gave a concert.*

# order

**Order** is the way that things are arranged. *Elsa arranged her dolls in order of size, from the smallest to the biggest.*

137

## order

**orders ordering ordered**
1 If someone **orders** you to do something, they tell you to do it.
2 If you **order** food in a restaurant, you say that you want it.

## ordinary

If something is **ordinary**, it is usual and not special.
*It was just an **ordinary** day.*

## organ

**organs**
1 An **organ** is a musical instrument with keys like a piano and lots of pipes of different sizes. When you press the keys, air is pushed through the pipes to make notes.
2 An **organ** is also a part of your body that does a particular job. Your heart and lungs are organs.

## organize

**organizes organizing organized**
When you **organize** something, you plan it so that it happens in the way that you want it to.
*We are **organizing** a party.*

## ornament

**ornaments**
An **ornament** is a small object that you put in a room because it looks nice. *Imogen arranged the **ornaments** on a shelf.*

## ostrich

**ostriches**
An **ostrich** is a very large bird with a long neck and long legs. Ostriches can run very fast, but cannot fly.

## other

1 **Other** means different. *Do you have any **other** games?*
2 **Other** also means the second of two things. *I can't find my **other** shoe.*

## otter

**otters**
An **otter** is an animal with brown fur and a long tail. Otters live near water, and catch fish to eat.

## ought

If you **ought to** do something, it is the right thing for you to do.
*You **ought to** practise the piano.*

# our

**Our** means belonging to us. *Have you met **our** new dog?*

# ours

If something belongs to us, then it is **ours**. *Your house is so tidy. **Ours** is falling apart.*

# out

1 **Out** means not inside, or from inside. *We went **out** for some fresh air. We took the books **out** of the box.*
■ *opposite* **in**
2 If a light or a fire **goes out**, it stops shining, or stops burning.

# outdoors

If you are **outdoors**, you are not in a building. *In the summer, we play **outdoors**.*
■ *opposite* **indoors**

# outing

**outings**
If you go on an **outing**, you visit somewhere, usually for a day. *Our class went on an **outing** to the zoo.*

# outline

**outlines**
An **outline** is a line around the edge of something. *Rosa drew the **outline** of a leaf.*

# outside

1 If something is **outside** a thing, it is close to it but not in it. *I left my shoes **outside** my bedroom.*
2 **Outside** also means outdoors. *We went **outside** as soon as it stopped raining.*

# oval

**ovals**
An **oval** is a shape like an egg.

# oven

**ovens**
An **oven** is the part of a cooker that you use for baking or roasting food.

# over

1 **Over** means above or on top of something. *Tim wore a jumper **over** his shirt.*
2 **Over** also means more than. *Lexi owns **over** 20 pairs of sunglasses.*
■ *opposite* **under**
3 If something is **over**, it is finished. *When the party was **over**, we went home.*
4 **Over** also means down. *Jake fell **over**.*

# overboard

If someone falls **overboard**, they fall off a boat into the water.

## overtake

**overtakes overtaking overtook overtaken**
When one vehicle **overtakes** another, it goes past it in the same direction. *Dad **overtook** a lorry on the motorway.*

## owe

**owes owing owed**
If you **owe** someone money, you have to pay them what you have borrowed.

## owl

**owls**
An **owl** is a bird with large eyes. Owls hunt at night.

## own

**1** If something is your **own**, it is yours. *He bought it with his **own** money.*
**2** If you are **on your own**, there is no one else with you.

## own

**owns owning owned**
If you **own** something, it belongs to you. *Richard **owns** two goldfish and three mice.*

# Pp

## pack

**packs packing packed**
When you **pack** a bag or a suitcase, you put things in it.

## package

**packages**
A **package** is a small parcel.

## packet

**packets**
A **packet** is a small container made from paper, card or plastic. *A **packet** of seeds.*

## pad

**pads**
**1** A **pad** has many pages joined together at one side. You can write or draw on a pad.
**2** A **pad** is also a thick piece of soft material.

## paddle

**paddles paddling paddled**
When you **paddle**, you walk in shallow water. *Pete and Lucy **paddled** in the sea.*

## page

**pages**
A **page** is a piece of paper in a book or a pad.

# paid

**Paid** comes from the word **pay**. *You must pay for your ticket before the show starts. We have already paid for ours.*

# pain

**Pain** is what you feel when you are hurt.

# painful

If something is **painful**, it hurts. *A painful knee.*

# paint

**paints**
Paint is a liquid that you use to put colour on things.

# paint

**paints painting painted**
1  When you **paint**, you use a brush and paints to make a picture.
2  If you **paint** a room, you put paint on its walls.

# pair

**pairs**
A **pair** is the name for two things that go together. *A pair of socks.*

# palace

**palaces**
A **palace** is a very large house where kings, queens or other very important people live.

# pale

**paler palest**
**Pale** colours have a lot of white in them. *Leona painted her room pale blue.*

# palm

**palms**
1  Your **palm** is the flat, inside surface of your hand. Your palm has many lines on it.
2  A **palm** is also a tall tree with large leaves at the top of its trunk. Palms grow in hot countries.

# pancake

**pancakes**
A **pancake** is a kind of thin, flat cake. You make pancakes by frying a mixture of milk, eggs and flour.

# panda

**pandas**
A **panda** is a black and white bear. Pandas live in China and eat bamboo.

a b c d e f g h i j k l m n o p q r s t u v w x y z

A
B
C
D
E
F
G
H
I
J
K
L
M
N
O
P
Q
R
S
T
U
V
W
X
Y
Z

## panic

**panics panicking panicked**
If you **panic**, you have a sudden feeling of fear. *Emma panicked when she couldn't find her mum.*

## pant

**pants panting panted**
When you **pant**, you breathe quickly and loudly because you are out of breath. *Jay was panting after his run.*

## panther

**panthers**
A **panther** is a leopard, usually a black one.

## pantomime

**pantomimes**
A **pantomime** is a play with songs and jokes. A pantomime usually tells the story of a fairy tale. *We went to see the pantomime Aladdin.*

## pants

**Pants** are underwear that cover your bottom.

## paper

**papers**
1 **Paper** is the material that is used for writing on, making books and wrapping things.
2 **Paper** is short for **newspaper**.

## parachute

**parachutes**
A **parachute** is a large piece of cloth with strings attached to it. Parachutes are used to drop people or things safely to the ground from a plane.

## parcel

**parcels**
A **parcel** is something wrapped in paper. Parcels are usually sent through the post.

## parent

**parents**
A **parent** is a mother or a father.

## park

**parks**
A **park** is a large piece of land where people can walk or play.

## park

**parks parking parked**
When someone **parks** their car, they leave it on the street or in a car park.

# parrot

**parrots**

A **parrot** is a brightly coloured bird with a curved beak. Some parrots can talk.

# part

**parts**

A **part** of a thing belongs to that thing. *Wheels and pedals are parts of a bicycle.*

# particular

**Particular** means this one and not any others. *This particular book is very helpful.*

# partner

**partners**

A **partner** is someone you do something with. *Darren is my dancing partner.*

# party

**parties**

If you have a **party**, you invite your friends to eat and have fun with you. *A birthday party.*

# pass

**passes passing passed**

**1** If you **pass** someone or something, you go past them. *We passed you as we drove home.*
**2** If you **pass** something to someone, you hand it to them.
**3** If you **pass** a ball to someone, you throw it or kick it to them.
**4** If you **pass** a test, you do well in it.

# passage

**passages**

A **passage** is a narrow path, usually between two buildings.

# passenger

**passengers**

A **passenger** is someone who travels in a vehicle and is not the driver.

# past

The **past** is the period of time that has already happened. *This story is set in the past when no one had televisions or telephones.*

# past

**Past** means by or beside. *The main road goes past our house.*

# paste

**Paste** is a soft, sticky mixture that you can spread. *Toothpaste.*

143

a b c d e f g h i j k l m n o p q r s t u v w x y z

A B C D E F G H I J K L M N O P Q R S T U V W X Y Z

## pastry

**Pastry** is a food made from flour, butter and water. You roll it flat and use it for making pies and tarts.

## pat

**pats patting patted**
If you **pat** something, you hit it gently with your hand. *Liam patted Fido on the back.*

## patch

**patches**
A **patch** is a small piece of cloth that you sew on clothes to cover a hole. *Jemima has a patch on her jeans.*

## path

**paths**
A **path** is a narrow road for people to walk along. *This path goes through the wood.*

## patient

**patients**
A **patient** is someone who is ill or hurt and is looked after by a doctor or a nurse.

## patient

Someone who is **patient** can wait for a long time without getting annoyed.
■ *opposite* **impatient**

## pattern

**patterns**
A **pattern** is the way that lines, shapes and colours are arranged. *I like the pattern on your curtains.*

## pause

**pauses pausing paused**
When you **pause**, you stop what you are doing for a short time.

## pavement

**pavements**
A **pavement** is a hard path beside a road. You walk on the pavement.

## paw

**paws**
A **paw** is an animal's foot. Dogs and cats have paws.

## pay

**pays paying paid**
If you **pay** someone, you give them money for something.

## pea

**peas**
A **pea** is a small, round, green vegetable. Peas grow in pods.

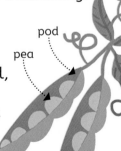

pod

pea

## peaceful
When it is **peaceful**, it is quiet.

## peach
**peaches**
A **peach** is a soft, round fruit with a furry skin. A peach has a stone in the middle of it.

## peacock
**peacocks**
A **peacock** is a large bird with long, colourful tail feathers.

## peak
**peaks**
1 The **peak** of a mountain is the point at its top.
2 The **peak** of a cap is the part at the front that sticks out.

## peanut
**peanuts**
A **peanut** is a small, oval nut. Peanuts have shells and grow under the ground.

## pear
**pears**
A **pear** is a juicy fruit. Pears are rounded at the bottom and get narrower towards the top.

## pebble
**pebbles**
A **pebble** is a smooth, round stone. You find pebbles on beaches.

## peculiar
If something is **peculiar**, it is unusual or strange. *Aunt Dottie has a **peculiar** habit of talking to flowers.*

## pedal
**pedals**
A **pedal** is a part of a bicycle. You press the pedals with your feet to make the bicycle move.

## peel
**peels peeling peeled**
When you **peel** a fruit or a vegetable, you remove the skin from it. *Ruth is **peeling** an apple.*

## peep
**peeps peeping peeped**
If you **peep** at something, you have a quick look at it. *Sophie **peeped** at the sleeping baby.*

A
B
C
D
E
F
G
H
I
J
K
L
M
N
O
P
Q
R
S
T
U
V
W
X
Y
Z

## peg
**pegs**
1 A **peg** is a hook that you use to hang things on.
2 You also use **pegs** to hold clothes on a washing line. Pegs are made from wood or plastic.

## pen
**pens**
You use a **pen** to write or draw in ink. Pens are made from plastic or metal.

## pencil
**pencils**
A **pencil** is a long, thin piece of wood with a black stick in the middle of it, called a lead. You use a pencil to write or draw.

## penguin
**penguins**
▲ *say pen-gwin*
A **penguin** is a black and white bird that lives in very cold places. Penguins cannot fly. They use their wings to swim.

## penny
**pennies** or **pence**
A **penny** is a coin. In Britain, there are 100 pennies in a pound.

## people
▲ *say pee-pull*
**People** are men, women and children.

## pepper
You shake **pepper** over your food to give it more flavour. Pepper tastes hot.

## perch
**perches perching perched**
**Perch** means to sit or stand on the edge of something. *The bird perched on the branch.*

## perfect
If something is **perfect**, it has nothing wrong with it at all. *Victoria practised the tune on her recorder until it was perfect.*

## performance
**performances**
A **performance** is something that you do in front of lots of people, such as singing, acting or playing an instrument.

## perfume
**perfumes**
**Perfume** is a liquid that smells nice. People put perfume on their skin.

# perhaps

You say **perhaps** when you mean that something is possible, but not certain. *Perhaps we'll see you this weekend.*

# period

**periods**
A **period** is a length of time. *Robert left the room for a short period.*

# permission

If you have **permission** to do something, you are allowed to do it. *Lisa was given permission to leave school early.*

# person

**people**
A **person** is a man, a woman or a child.

# persuade

**persuades persuading persuaded**
If you **persuade** someone to do something, you make them agree to do it. *Amy persuaded me to wait for her.*

# pest

**pests**
A **pest** is a person or an animal that causes trouble. *Wasps can be terrible pests.*

# pet

**pets**
A **pet** is an animal that lives with you at home. Cats and dogs are common pets. *Joel keeps rabbits as pets.*

# petal

**petals**
**Petals** are the colourful parts of a flower. *This daisy has pink petals.*

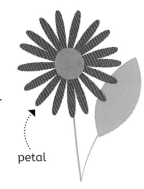

petal

# petrol

**Petrol** is a liquid that you put into a vehicle to make it run.

# phone

**phones**
**Phone** is short for **telephone**.

# photograph

**photographs**
A **photograph** is a picture that you take with a camera. Photo is short for photograph.

a b c d e f g h i j k l m n o p q r s t u v w x y z

A B C D E F G H I J K L M N O P Q R S T U V W X Y Z

# piano
**pianos**
A **piano** is a large musical instrument with a row of black and white keys. You press the keys with your fingers to play different notes.

# pick
**picks picking picked**
1 When you **pick** something, you choose it. *Pick any cake you want.*
2 If you **pick** fruit or flowers, you take them from a plant or a tree.
3 If you **pick up** something, you lift it up. *Kim picked up the kitten.*

# picnic
**picnics**
A **picnic** is a meal that you take with you to eat outdoors.

# picture
**pictures**
A **picture** is a painting, a drawing or a photograph.

# pie
**pies**
A **pie** is a pastry case filled with meat, vegetables or fruit. Pies are baked in an oven.

# piece
**pieces**
A **piece** of something is a part of it. *A piece of the jigsaw is missing.*

# pier
**piers**
A **pier** is a long platform that is built out over the sea. Piers often have games and rides on them.

# pig
**pigs**
A **pig** is a farm animal with a fat body and short legs. Pigs are kept for their meat.

# pigeon
**pigeons**
▲ say *pij-in*
A **pigeon** is a grey bird with a rounded body and a small head.

# pile

**piles**

A **pile** is a lot of things that have been put on top of each other. *A pile of clothes.*

# pill

**pills**

A **pill** is a small, dry piece of medicine. People swallow pills when they are ill to help them get better.

# pillow

**pillows**

A **pillow** is a kind of cushion that you rest your head on when you are lying in bed.

# pilot

**pilots**

A **pilot** is someone who flies a plane. *The pilot flew his plane over the woods and fields.*

# pin

**pins**

A **pin** is a small, thin piece of metal with a point at one end. You use pins to hold things together.

# pinch

**pinches pinching pinched**

If you **pinch** someone, you squeeze their skin between your thumb and finger.

# pineapple

**pineapples**

A **pineapple** is a large, oval fruit with a tough skin and pointed leaves at the top.

# pink

**Pink** is the colour that you make when you mix red and white. Strawberry ice cream is pink.

# pipe

**pipes**

A **pipe** is a long tube that carries gas or liquids.

# pirate

**pirates**

A **pirate** is someone who attacks ships at sea and steals things from them.

# pit

**pits**

A **pit** is a deep hole in the ground.

a b c d e f g h i j k l m n o p q r s t u v w x y z

## pitch

**pitches**
A **pitch** is an area of ground where people play sports such as football.

## pity

**pities pitying pitied**
If you **pity** someone, you feel sorry for them.

## pizza

**pizzas**
▲ *say peet-sah*
A **pizza** is a flat piece of bread with tomatoes and cheese on top. You can also have vegetables, meat or fish on pizzas. Pizzas are usually round and are baked in an oven.
*A slice of pizza.*

## place

**places**
A **place** is somewhere. Places can be very big, like a country, or very small, like a cupboard.
*Africa is a very hot place.*
*Can you find a place to put your mug?*

## place

**places placing placed**
If you **place** a thing somewhere, you put it there. *Place the vase in the middle of the table.*

## plain

**plainer plainest**
**1** Something that is **plain** is ordinary, or not decorated. *Rory prefers plain food. I have plain curtains in my room.*
**2** If something is **plain**, it is clear and easy to understand. *Gareth made it plain that he did not like peas.*

## plan

**plans planning planned**
If you **plan** something, you decide how you will do it. *We planned the treasure hunt carefully.*

## plane

**planes**
**Plane** is short for **aeroplane**.

## planet

**planets**
A **planet** is a huge, round object that moves around the Sun. The Earth is a planet.

## plank

**planks**
A **plank** is a long, flat piece of wood.

# plant

**plants**

A **plant** is a living thing that grows in soil or in water. Trees and flowers are plants.

# plaster

**plasters**

1  A **plaster** is a sticky strip with a soft pad in the middle, that you use to protect a cut.

2  A **plaster** is also a hard case that holds the parts of a broken bone together until they are mended.

# plastic

**Plastic** is a material that can be shaped to make bottles, buckets and many other things.

plastic bucket

# plate

**plates**

A **plate** is a flat dish that you put food on.

# platform

**platforms**

1  A **platform** is the place where you stand to wait for a train.

2  A **platform** is also a raised area, often used as a stage.

# play

**plays**

A **play** is a story that you act out.

# play

**plays playing played**

1  When you **play**, you do something for fun. *The boys are playing in the park.*

2  If you **play** a sport, you take part in it. *Alex is playing football.*

3  If you **play** a musical instrument, you use it to make music.

*Charlotte plays the recorder.*

# playground

**playgrounds**

A **playground** is a place where you can play outdoors. Playgrounds often have swings and other play equipment.

# pleasant

If something is **pleasant**, you enjoy it. *We had a pleasant walk.*

a b c d e f g h i j k l m n o p q r s t u v w x y z

## please

**pleases pleasing pleased**
If you **please** someone, you make them happy. *Carlo **pleased** his mother by tidying his room.*

## please

You say **please** when you ask for something in a polite way. ***Please** may I have an apple?*

## plenty

If there is **plenty** of something, there is more than enough of it. *We have **plenty** of food for our picnic.*

## plough

**ploughs**
▲ *rhymes with* **cow**
A **plough** is a set of sharp blades that is pulled by a tractor. Ploughs are used to dig up earth in fields.

## pluck

**plucks plucking plucked**
When you **pluck** something, you pull on it with your fingers. *Amy **plucked** the guitar string. Suzy **plucked** her eyebrows.*

## plug

**plugs**
1 A **plug** is a round piece of plastic or rubber used to keep water in a sink or a bath.
2 A **plug** is also a small object that connects a machine to the electric power.

## plum

**plums**
A **plum** is a soft fruit with yellow, red or purple skin. A plum has a stone in the middle of it.

## plus

**Plus** means add. The sign for plus is +. *Three **plus** four equals seven.*

3+4=7

■ *opposite* **minus**

## pocket

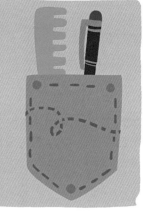

**pockets**
A **pocket** is a small bag that is sewn into clothes. You can keep things in your pockets.

## pocket money

**Pocket money** is money that your parents give you to spend.

## pod

**pods**
A **pod** is a part of a plant that contains seeds. Peas and most beans grow in pods.

# poem

**poems**

A **poem** is a piece of writing. Poems usually have short lines and often have words that rhyme.

There was an old man
    with a beard
Who said, "It is just as I feared!
Two owls and a hen,
    Four larks and a wren,
Have all built their nests
    in my beard!"
                — Edward Lear

# point

**points**

**1** A **point** is the sharp end of something. *A pencil point.*

**2** A **point** is also part of a score in a game or a competition. *Our team got seven points.*

# point

**points pointing pointed**

If you **point at** something, you use your finger to show where it is. *Karma pointed at the squirrels in the bushes.*

# poisonous

If you eat something **poisonous**, it can make you very ill or even kill you.

# polar bear

**polar bears**

A **polar bear** is a large, white bear that lives near the North Pole.

# pole

**poles**

A **pole** is a long, thin piece of wood or metal. *A flagpole.*

# police

▲ *say puh-leece*

The **police** protect people and make sure that the law is obeyed.

# polish

**polishes polishing polished**

When you **polish** something, you rub it to make it shiny. *Jayden polished his dad's car.*

# polite

**politer politest**

A **polite** person has good manners and thinks about other people's feelings.

■ *opposite* **rude**

A B C D E F G H I J K L M N O P Q R S T U V W X Y Z

## pollution

**Pollution** is damage to the environment. Traffic fumes and litter are types of pollution.

## pond
**ponds**
A **pond** is a small area of water.

## pony
**ponies**
A **pony** is a type of horse that is small even when it is fully grown.

## pool
**pools**
A **pool** is a small area of water.

paddling pool

## poor
**poorer poorest**
1 People who are **poor** do not have much money.
■ *opposite* **rich**
2 If something is **poor**, it is not very good. *Poor handwriting.*

## pop
**pops popping popped**
If something **pops**, it explodes with a small bang. *The balloon popped when the cat jumped on it. She had such a fright!*

## popular
Someone who is **popular** is liked by many people. *Jodie is very popular. She has lots of friends.*

## pork
**Pork** is a type of meat that comes from a pig.

## porridge
**Porridge** is a thick, sticky food made from oats cooked in milk or water.

## port
**ports**
A **port** is a town with a harbour.

## position
**positions**
1 The **position** of something is the place where it is. *Sarah's house is in a wonderful position, just next to the park.*
2 Someone's **position** is the way that they are standing or sitting.

## possession
**possessions**
A **possession** is something that you own. *Don't leave any of your possessions on the coach.*

## possible

If something is **possible**, it can happen or it can be done. *It is possible to reach Mars, but it will be hard to get there.*
■ *opposite* **impossible**

## post

**posts**
A **post** is a long, thick piece of wood, metal or concrete that is fixed in the ground.

## post

**posts posting posted**
1 If you **post** a letter, you put it in a postbox to be sent to someone.
2 If you **post** a comment or a picture on the internet, you put it on a website where lots of people can see it.

## postcard

**postcards**
A **postcard** is a card that you post without an envelope. Postcards usually have a picture on one side.

## poster

**posters**
A **poster** is a large picture or notice that is stuck on a wall. *Callum has covered his bedroom wall with posters.*

## post office

**post offices**
A **post office** is a place where you can buy stamps and post letters and parcels.

## pot

**pots**
1 A **pot** is a deep, round container. People use pots for cooking food.
2 A **pot** is also a container for a plant.

## potato

**potatoes**
A **potato** is a rounded vegetable that grows under the ground.

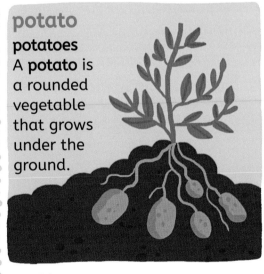

## pottery

**Pottery** is a name for objects that are made out of clay, such as bowls and mugs.

155

# pound

**pounds**
A **pound** is a unit of money.
In Britain, a pound is made up
of 100 pennies. The sign
for a pound is £.

# pour

**pours pouring poured**
When you **pour** a liquid, you tip
it carefully out of its container.

# powder

**powders**
**Powder** is made up of lots
of very tiny grains. Flour is
a powder.

# power

1  **Power** is the strength and
ability to do something. *The
truck had the **power** to tow
our car out of the mud.*
2  If someone has **power** over
other people or things, they
control them.
3  **Power** is another name for
electricity. *Our **power** was
cut off in the storm.*

# practise

**practises practising practised**
If you **practise** something, you
do it again and again so
that you get better at it.
*Abby **practises** the
trumpet every day.*

# precious

1  A **precious**
object is worth
a lot of money.
*Princess Aurora has
a chest of **precious** jewels.*
2  Something that is **precious** is
very important or special to you.

# prefer

**prefers preferring preferred**
If you **prefer** something, you like
it better than another thing.
*I **prefer** apples to oranges.*

# prepare

**prepares preparing prepared**
If you **prepare**, you get ready.
*Lydia is **preparing** for
her holiday.*

# present

**presents**
1  A **present** is something special
that you give to someone.
2  The **present** is the time now.
*The story begins in the **present**.*

# president

**presidents**
A **president** is someone who
runs a country.

# press
**presses pressing pressed**
If you **press** something, you push it with your finger. *Press this button to turn on the television.*

# pretend
**pretends pretending pretended**
When you **pretend**, you act as if something were true, even though it is not. *Sam pretended that he was asleep. Ella is pretending to be a frog.*

# pretty
▲ *rhymes with* **pity**
**prettier prettiest**
Something or someone that is **pretty** is nice to look at.

# prevent
**prevents preventing prevented**
If you **prevent** something, you stop it from happening. *Jessica acted quickly to prevent an accident.*

# prey
**Prey** is a name for the creatures that birds and animals hunt and eat. *The tiger chased after its prey.*

# price
**prices**
The **price** of something is how much money it costs. *What's the price of this bag?*

# prick
**pricks pricking pricked**
If you **prick** yourself, something sharp makes a tiny hole in your skin. *Coral has pricked her finger.*

# prince
**princes**
A **prince** is the son of a king or a queen.

# princess
**princesses**
A **princess** is the daughter of a king or a queen.

# print
**prints printing printed**
1 When someone **prints** something, they use a machine called a printer to put words or pictures onto paper. *Mrs Parsnip printed my story for me.*
2 When you **print**, you write with letters that are not joined up.

# prison
**prisons**
A **prison** is a place where people are kept as a punishment because they have not obeyed the law.

## private

If something is **private**, it is only for particular people. *A **private** letter.*
■ opposite **public**

## prize

**prizes**
You win a **prize** as a reward for doing something well. *Carl won a cup as his **prize** for coming first in the race.*

## probably

If something will **probably** happen, there is more chance that it will happen than it won't. *It will **probably** rain again tomorrow.*

## problem

**problems**
A **problem** is something difficult that you need to find an answer to. *We have a **problem** with our kitten. She keeps running away.*

## produce

**produces producing produced**
1 When you **produce** something, you make it. *The chocolate factory **produces** all kinds of sweets.*
2 If you **produce** something, you get it out so that people can see it. *Ginger **produced** a mouse from his pocket.*

## program

**programs**
A **program** is a set of instructions that tells a computer how to work.

## programme

**programmes**
1 A **programme** is something that you watch on television or hear on the radio. *A nature **programme**.*
2 A **programme** is also a small book or list that tells you about a play or a concert.

## progress

When you **make progress**, you get better or move forwards. *Lucy is **making** good **progress** at school. The explorers **made** slow **progress** through the jungle.*

## project

**projects**
When you do a **project**, you find out about a subject.

*Ewan and Ravi are doing a **project** on sound.*

## promise

**promises promising promised**
When you **promise**, you say that you will really do something. *Molly **promised** to be on time.*

## proper

**Proper** means right or correct. *Is this the **proper** way to get on a horse?*

## protect

**protects protecting protected**
When you **protect** someone or something, you keep them safe.

Jo **protected** her puppy from the rain.

## proud

**prouder proudest**
If you feel **proud**, you feel pleased about what you have done. *Jessie is **proud** of her cake.*

## prove

**proves proving proved**
When you **prove** something, you show that it is true.

## provide

**provides providing provided**
When you **provide** something, you give people what they need. *The hotel **provides** lunch.*

## public

If something is **public**, everyone can use it. *A **public** park.*
■ opposite **private**

## pudding

**puddings**
A **pudding** is a sweet food that you eat at the end of a meal.

## puddle

**puddles**
A **puddle** is a small pool of water. You see puddles on the ground when it has been raining.

puddle ......

## pull

**pulls pulling pulled**
If you **pull** something, you move it towards you. *Richard **pulled** his suitcase out of the cupboard.*

## pump

**pumps**
You use a **pump** to push air or liquid into something. *A bicycle **pump**.*

## punch

**punches punching punched**
If you **punch** something, you hit it with your fist.

a b c d e f g h i j k l m n o p q r s t u v w x y z

## punish
**punishes punishing punished**
If someone **punishes** you, they do something to you because you have been naughty.
*Mum **punished** me for being rude by sending me to bed.*

## pupil
**pupils**
A **pupil** is someone who learns something, usually in a school.
*There are 30 **pupils** in my class.*

## puppet
**puppets**
A **puppet** is a doll that can be made to move. Some puppets are like gloves and you move them with your fingers. Others have strings that you can pull.

## puppy
**puppies**
A **puppy** is a young dog.

## purple
**Purple** is the colour that you make when you mix red and blue.

## purpose
▲ say **pur-pus**
If you do something **on purpose**, you mean to do it. *Matt kicked his sister **on purpose** to see if she would cry.*

## purr
**purrs purring purred**
When a cat **purrs**, it makes a low sound in its throat to show that it is happy.

## purse
**purses**
A **purse** is a small bag that you keep money in.

## push
**pushes pushing pushed**
If you **push** something, you move it in front of you or away from you. *Daniel **pushed** his bike up the hill.*

## put
**puts putting put**
When you **put** a thing somewhere, you move it to that place. *Please **put** the milk in the fridge.*

# puzzle

**puzzles**

A **puzzle** is a type of game where you have to work out an answer.

|   | c | o | l | d |
|---|---|---|---|---|
| 1 | c | o | r | d |
| 2 | w | o | r | d |
| 3 | w | o | r | m |
|   | w | a | r | m |

**Can you get from cold to warm in three words?**

Answer the clues and fill in the boxes. For each answer, change just one letter from the word above.

**CLUES**

1 A type of string
2 A group of letters
3 A creature that lives in the ground

# pyjamas

**Pyjamas** are the matching shirt and trousers that some people wear in bed.

# Qq

# quack

**quacks quacking quacked**

When a duck **quacks**, it opens its beak and makes a loud sound.

# quantity

**quantities**

A **quantity** is an amount or a number. *A large quantity of sand.*

# quarrel

**quarrels quarrelling quarrelled**

When people **quarrel**, they argue and get angry with each other. *The boys quarrelled over who should go first.*

# quarry

**quarries**

A **quarry** is a place where stone is dug out of the ground.

# quarter

**quarters**

If something is cut into **quarters**, it is cut into four pieces of the same size.

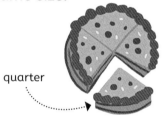

quarter

# queen

**queens**

A **queen** is a woman who rules a country. Queens come from royal families and are not chosen by the people.

## question

**questions**

A **question** is what you ask when you want to know something.

## queue

**queues**

▲ *say* **kyoo**

A **queue** is a line of people who are waiting for something. *We waited in the* **queue** *for the bus.*

## quick

**quicker quickest**

1 Something that is **quick** moves at a great speed.
2 If something is **quick**, it only lasts for a short time. *Miranda had a* **quick** *look round the house.*

## quiet

**quieter quietest**

Someone who is being **quiet** does not make much noise.

■ *opposite* **loud**

## quite

1 **Quite** means a bit. *It's* **quite** *warm outside.*
2 **Quite** also means completely. *I haven't* **quite** *finished my book.*

## quiz

**quizzes**

A **quiz** is a game or a test to find out how much you know. You have to answer questions in a quiz.

# Rr

## rabbit

**rabbits**

A **rabbit** is a small, furry animal with long ears and a short tail. Wild rabbits live in holes under the ground called burrows.

## race

**races**

A **race** is a competition to find out who can go fastest. *A relay* **race**.

## racket

**rackets**

A **racket** is a bat with strings stretched across it. *A tennis* **racket**.

## radiator

**radiators**

A **radiator** is used to heat a room. Radiators are made of metal and are usually filled with hot water.

## radio
**radios**
A **radio** is a machine that receives signals through the air and sends out sounds. You can listen to music and news on a radio.

## raft
**rafts**
A **raft** is a kind of flat boat. Rafts are often made from planks of wood that are fixed together.

## rag
**rags**
A **rag** is a piece of old cloth. You use rags to clean things.

## raid
**raids**
A **raid** is a sudden attack. *An air raid.*

## rail
**rails**
1  A **rail** is a bar that you can hold on to. *Hold on to the rail as you climb the stairs.*
2  **Rails** are long metal bars that trains and trams run on.
3  If you go somewhere **by rail**, you travel on a train.

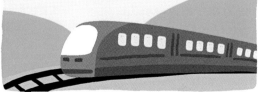

## railway
**railways**
A **railway** is a track for trains to travel along.

## rain
**rains raining rained**
When it **rains**, drops of water fall from the clouds.

## rainbow
**rainbows**
A **rainbow** is a curved band of different colours that you sometimes see in the sky. Rainbows appear when the Sun shines while it is raining.

## raise
**raises raising raised**
If you **raise** something, you lift it up. *Laura raised her hand to answer the question.*

## rake
**rakes**
A **rake** is a garden tool with a long handle and metal teeth. You use a rake to collect leaves.

## ran
**Ran** comes from the word **run**. *Kitty runs for the school team. She ran in five races last month.*

Some words that begin with an "r" sound, such as **wrap**, are spelt **"wr"**.

## rare
**rarer rarest**
If something is **rare**, you do not see it very often.
*A **rare** butterfly.*
■ *opposite* **common**

## raspberry
**raspberries**
A **raspberry** is a small, red fruit. Raspberries are soft and juicy and grow on bushes.

## rat
**rats**
A **rat** is a small animal with a long tail and sharp teeth. Rats sometimes spread disease.

## rather
**1** If you would **rather** do something, you want to do it more than something else. *I'd **rather** go to the beach than do my homework.*
**2 Rather** means more than a little. *Henrietta is **rather** clever.*

## raw
Food that is **raw** has not been cooked. ***Raw** carrots.*

## reach
**reaches reaching reached**
**1** When you **reach** for something, you stretch out your hand to touch it. *Tia **reached** for the light.*
**2** When you **reach** a place, you arrive there. *It was very late when we **reached** the hotel.*

## read
**reads reading read**
**1** When you **read**, you look at words and understand what they mean. *Jack **read** his new book.*
**2** When you **read** something to someone, you say it out loud. *Skye is **reading** to her brother.*

## ready
If you are **ready**, you can do something now. *I'm **ready** to go.*

## real
**1** Something that is **real** is true.
**2** Something that is **real** is not a copy. *A **real** diamond.*

## really
**1 Really** means that something is true. *Men **really** have walked on the Moon.*
**2 Really** also means very. *Georgia was **really** annoyed that she'd missed the bus.*

## reason

**reasons**
The **reason** for something is why it has happened. *The reason I'm late is that my alarm clock didn't work.*

## receive

**receives receiving received**
If you **receive** something, you get something that is given to you or sent to you. *I received your present this morning.*

## recent

Something that is **recent** happened a short time ago.

## recipe

**recipes**
▲ say **ress-ippy**
A **recipe** is a set of instructions that tells you how to make something to eat or drink.

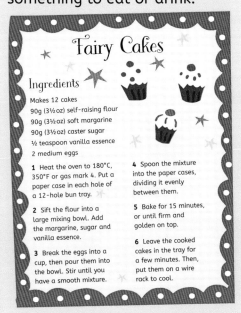

Fairy Cakes

Ingredients
Makes 12 cakes
90g (3½oz) self-raising flour
90g (3½oz) soft margarine
90g (3½oz) caster sugar
½ teaspoon vanilla essence
2 medium eggs

**1** Heat the oven to 180°C, 350°F or gas mark 4. Put a paper case in each hole of a 12-hole bun tray.

**2** Sift the flour into a large mixing bowl. Add the margarine, sugar and vanilla essence.

**3** Break the eggs into a cup, then pour them into the bowl. Stir until you have a smooth mixture.

**4** Spoon the mixture into the paper cases, dividing it evenly between them.

**5** Bake for 15 minutes, or until firm and golden on top.

**6** Leave the cooked cakes in the tray for a few minutes. Then, put them on a wire rack to cool.

## recite

**recites reciting recited**
When you **recite** something, such as a poem, you remember it and say it aloud.

## recognize

**recognizes recognizing recognized**
If you **recognize** someone, you see them and know who they are. *I recognized Dylan easily.*

## record

**records recording recorded**
If you **record** some music or a television programme, you make a copy of it.

## recorder

**recorders**
A **recorder** is a musical instrument. You blow into a recorder and cover the holes with your fingers to make different notes.

## recover

**recovers recovering recovered**
When you **recover**, you feel better again.

## rectangle

**rectangles**
A **rectangle** is a shape with four sides and four corners. It has two long sides of the same length and two short sides of the same length.

## recycle

**recycles recycling recycled**
If you **recycle** something, you use it again, or you use it to make something new. *Our class is collecting rubbish to recycle.*

## red

**Red** is a colour. Blood and tomatoes are red.

## reduce

**reduces reducing reduced**
If you **reduce** something, you make it smaller. *The toy shop has reduced its prices.*

## referee

**referees**
A **referee** makes sure that the players obey the rules of a game.

*The referee blew his whistle.*

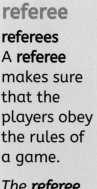

## reflection

**reflections**
You see a **reflection** when you look in a mirror.

## refreshments

**Refreshments** are food and drink. *There will be refreshments after the concert.*

## refuse

**refuses refusing refused**
If you **refuse** to do something that someone has asked you to, you say that you will not do it.
■ opposite **agree**

## register

**registers**
A **register** is a list of names. Registers are used in schools to check that everybody is there.

## rehearse

**rehearses rehearsing rehearsed**
When you **rehearse**, you practise something before a performance. *We have been rehearsing for the concert all week.*

# reindeer

**reindeer**
A **reindeer** is a kind of deer. Reindeer have large horns called antlers. They live in very cold places.

# reins

**Reins** are the leather straps that you use to control a horse.

# relative

**relatives**
A **relative** is a member of your family.

# relax

**relaxes relaxing relaxed**
When you **relax**, you rest and stop worrying. *Ben relaxes by listening to music.*

# remain

**remains remaining remained**
If you **remain** in a place, you stay there. *Clare remained at home while we went to the park.*

# remember

**remembers remembering remembered**
When you **remember** something, it comes back into your mind. *Simon has remembered where he left his jacket.*
■ *opposite* **forget**

# remind

**reminds reminding reminded**
If you **remind** someone about something, you help them to remember it. *Joshua reminded me to send Emily's birthday card.*

# remote control

**remote controls**
You use a **remote control** to control a machine such as a television from a distance.

# remove

**removes removing removed**
When you **remove** something, you take it away. *I didn't recognize Sue until she removed her mask.*

# rent

**rents renting rented**
If you **rent** a house, you pay money to its owner so that you can live in it.

# repair

**repairs repairing repaired**
When you **repair** something, you mend it so that it can be used again.

a b c d e f g h i j k l m n o p q **r** s t u v w x y z

# repeat

**repeats repeating repeated**
If you **repeat** something, you say it again or do it again. *Please* **repeat** *your name so that I can write it down.*

# replace

**replaces replacing replaced**
1 If you **replace** something, you put another thing in its place. *Kian* **replaced** *the broken vase with a new one.*
2 **Replace** also means to put something back where it came from. *Shazia* **replaced** *the book on the shelf.*

# reply

**replies replying replied**
When you **reply**, you give an answer. *Thomas* **replied** *to Lucy's invitation.*

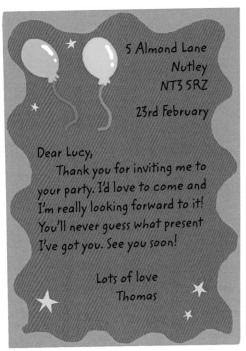

5 Almond Lane
Nutley
NT3 5RZ

23rd February

Dear Lucy,
    Thank you for inviting me to your party. I'd love to come and I'm really looking forward to it! You'll never guess what present I've got you. See you soon!

Lots of love
Thomas

# reptile

**reptiles**
A **reptile** is an animal with dry, scaly skin. Most reptiles lay eggs. Crocodiles, snakes and lizards are reptiles.

lizard

# require

**requires requiring required**
If you **require** something, you need it. *You will* **require** *paper, scissors and glue to make this model boat.*

# rescue

**rescues rescuing rescued**
If you **rescue** someone, you help them to escape from danger.

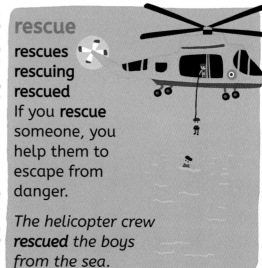

*The helicopter crew* **rescued** *the boys from the sea.*

# responsible

1 If you are **responsible** for something, you are the one who has to do it. *I am* **responsible** *for feeding Tinkerbell.*
2 A **responsible** person is sensible and can be trusted.

## rest

**The rest** is what is left. *I ate **the rest** of the pizza the next day.*

## rest

**rests resting rested**
When you **rest**, you sit down or lie down because you are tired.

## restaurant

**restaurants**
A **restaurant** is a place with tables and chairs, where you buy and eat meals.

> Some words that begin with an "r" sound, such as **wrestle**, **wrist** and **write**, are spelt "**wr**".

## result

**results**
A **result** is something that happens because of something else. *I got lost and I was late as a **result**.*

## return

**returns returning returned**
1 If you **return** to a place, you come back to it.
2 If you **return** something, you give it back. *Theo **returned** the books that he had borrowed.*

## reverse

**reverses reversing reversed**
When someone **reverses** a car, they drive it backwards.

## revolting

If something is **revolting**, it makes you feel sick.
*A **revolting** smell.*

## reward

**rewards**
A **reward** is something that you are given because you have done something good.

## rhinoceros

**rhinoceroses**
A **rhinoceros** is a large, heavy animal with thick, wrinkled skin. Rhinoceroses have one or two horns on their noses.

## rhyme

**rhymes rhyming rhymed**
Words that **rhyme** end with the same sound. Fight, kite and might all rhyme.

## rhythm

**rhythms**
A **rhythm** is a repeated pattern of sound. Music and poems have rhythm.

a b c d e f g h i j k l m n o p q **r** s t u v w x y z

## rib

**ribs**

A **rib** is one of the bones that curve round from your back to your chest. Your ribs protect your heart and your lungs.

## ribbon

**ribbons**

A **ribbon** is a long piece of material that you tie around things. *Alice tied a ribbon around the parcel.*

## rice

**Rice** is a food that comes from a type of grass plant. Rice grains can be cooked and eaten.

## rich

**richer richest**

People who are **rich** have a lot of money.

■ *opposite* **poor**

## riddle

**riddles**

A **riddle** is a question with a surprising and clever answer.

## ride

**rides**

1 A **ride** is a journey in a vehicle or on an animal. *It's a long car ride to my uncle's house.*

2 A **ride** at the fair is a machine that spins you round or turns you upside down.

## ride

**rides riding rode ridden**

If you **ride** a bicycle or a horse, you sit on it and move along.

## ridiculous

Something that is **ridiculous** is very silly. *Andrew looks ridiculous in his mum's hat.*

## right

1 Something that is **right** is correct and does not have any mistakes in it.

■ *opposite* **wrong**

2 If you do something that is **right**, you do something good or fair.

■ *opposite* **wrong**

3 You have a **right** hand and a left hand. Most people draw with their right hand.

■ *opposite* **left**

## ring

**rings**

A **ring** is a band that you wear on your finger.

# ring
**rings ringing rang rung**
**1** When you **ring** someone, you call them on the telephone.
**2** When a bell **rings**, it makes a loud noise.

# ringtone
**ringtones**
A **ringtone** is the sound or tune a mobile phone makes when someone calls it.

# rink
**rinks**
A **rink** is a place where you can ice-skate or roller-skate.

# rinse
**rinses rinsing rinsed**
When you **rinse** something, you clean it in water.

# rip
**rips ripping ripped**
If you **rip** something, you tear it. *Evan **ripped** his trousers on the fence.*

# ripe
**riper ripest**
If food is **ripe**, it is ready to be eaten. ***Ripe** tomatoes.*

# rise
**rises rising rose risen**
When something **rises**, it moves up. *The balloon **rose** into the air.*

# risk
**risks**
If you take a **risk**, you do something that you know could be dangerous. *Robert took a **risk** when he jumped backwards into the pool.*

# river
**rivers**
A **river** is a large amount of water running across land. Rivers have banks on either side. They run into lakes or seas.

# road
**roads**
A **road** is a hard strip of ground that goes from one place to another. Vehicles travel on roads.

# roar
**roars roaring roared**
When an animal **roars**, it makes a loud, low sound in its throat. *The lion **roared**.*

## roast

**roasts roasting roasted**
When you **roast** food, you cook it in a hot oven. *Mum has roasted a chicken for lunch.*

## rob

**robs robbing robbed**
If you **rob** someone, you steal things from them. *Three men robbed the bank yesterday. We were robbed.*

## robin

**robins**
A **robin** is a small bird with a red chest.

## robot

**robots**
A **robot** is a machine that can do some jobs that people do. Some robots look a bit like people.

## rock

**rocks**
1 **Rock** is the very hard part of the Earth. Mountains are made of rock.
2 A **rock** is a large stone.

## rock

**rocks rocking rocked**
When you **rock**, you move gently backwards and forwards or from side to side.

## rocket

**rockets**
1 A **rocket** is a spacecraft that travels very fast. Rockets take astronauts into space.
2 A **rocket** is also a type of firework.

## rode

**Rode** comes from the word **ride**. *Lucy rides her pony every day. She rode for hours yesterday.*

## roll

**rolls**
1 A **roll** is a small, round piece of bread. *A cheese roll.*
2 A **roll** is also a long piece of paper or tape wrapped around itself many times.

## roll

**rolls rolling rolled**
When something **rolls**, it moves by turning over and over. *The ball rolled down the hill.*

## roller skate

**roller skates**
**Roller skates** are boots with wheels on, used for skating.

Some words that begin with an "r" sound, such as **wrong** and **wrote**, are spelt "**wr**".

## roof

**roofs**
A **roof** is the top of a building.

## room

**rooms**
1 A **room** is an area inside a building. Rooms usually have four walls and a door.
2 If there is **room** for something, there is enough space for it.

## root

**roots**
A **root** is the part of a plant that grows under the ground. Water travels up the root to the rest of the plant.

## rope

**ropes**
A **rope** is made of lots of threads twisted together. Ropes are often used for pulling things.

## rose

**roses**
A **rose** is a flower with thorns on its stem. Roses often smell nice.

## rose

**Rose** comes from the word **rise**. *Laura watched the balloon rise. It rose high into the sky.*

## rough

**rougher roughest**
▲ *rhymes with* **stuff**
1 If something is **rough**, it is not smooth. *Rough skin.*
2 Someone who is **rough** is not gentle. *Don't be so rough, you're hurting me!*
3 A **rough** answer is not exactly correct.

## round

**rounder roundest**
Something that is **round** has a shape like a circle or a ball.

## row

**rows**
1 A **row** is a line of people or things. *A row of chairs.*
▲ *rhymes with* **go**
2 A **row** is an argument.
▲ *rhymes with* **how**

## row

**rows rowing rowed**
▲ *rhymes with* **go**
When you **row**, you use oars to make a boat move through water.

## royal

Someone who is **royal** is part of the family of a king or a queen.

## rub

**rubs rubbing rubbed**
If you **rub** something, you move your hand or a cloth backwards and forwards over it. You often rub things to make them clean.

## rubber

**rubbers**
**1 Rubber** is a strong material that can bend and stretch. Rubber is used to make tyres, balls, boots and rubber bands.

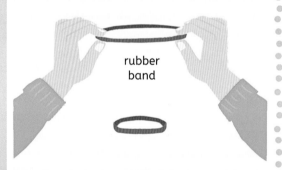

rubber band

**2** A **rubber** is a soft block that you rub over pencil marks to remove them.

## rubbish

**1 Rubbish** is the name for things that you throw away because you don't want them any more.
**2** If you say that something is **rubbish**, you think it is very bad or isn't true. *That painting is **rubbish**. Don't talk **rubbish**, George.*

## rude

**ruder rudest**
**Rude** people have bad manners and are not polite. *It is **rude** to speak with your mouth full of food.*
■ *opposite* **polite**

## rug

**rugs**
A **rug** is a small carpet that covers part of a floor.

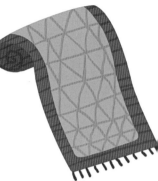

## rugby

**Rugby** is a game with an oval ball played by two teams. Each team tries to carry the ball across a line or kick it over a bar.

## ruin

**ruins ruining ruined**
If you **ruin** something, you spoil it completely. *My brother has **ruined** my picture by scribbling on it.*

## rule

**rules**
A **rule** tells you what you can or cannot do. Games have rules that you must obey.

## rule

**rules ruling ruled**
Someone who **rules** a country is in charge of it.

## ruler

**rulers**

1 A **ruler** is a flat piece of plastic, wood or metal with straight edges. You use a ruler to draw straight lines or to measure things.

2 A **ruler** is also someone who is in charge of a country.

## run

**runs running ran run**
1 When you **run**, you move quickly, using your legs.

*Luke **ran** for the bus.*

2 When water **runs**, it moves. *The river **runs** into the sea.*
3 When a machine **runs**, it works. *This radio **runs** on batteries.*
4 If someone **runs** something, they are in charge of it.

## rung

**Rung** comes from the word **ring**. *Tim wants you to ring him. He has **rung** you twice today already.*

## runway

**runways**
A **runway** is a strip of land where planes take off and land.

## rush

**rushes rushing rushed**
When you **rush**, you hurry or you do something quickly. *We're late, so we'll have to **rush**.*

# Ss

## sack

**sacks**
A **sack** is a large bag made from strong cloth or plastic. Sacks are used for carrying and storing things.

## sad

**sadder saddest**
If you are **sad**, you feel unhappy. *Ollie was **sad** when his fish died.*
■ opposite **happy**

Some other words for **sad** are **unhappy, depressed, upset, miserable** and **glum**.

## saddle

**saddles**
A **saddle** is a seat for a rider on a horse or a bicycle.

a b c d e f g h i j k l m n o p q r s t u v w x y z

## safe

**safer safest**

1 If you are **safe**, nothing bad can happen to you.
2 If something is **safe**, it cannot hurt you. *Dad mended my bike so that it was* **safe** *to ride.*

## said

▲ *rhymes with* **bed**
**Said** comes from the word **say**. *Mum asked us to say what we wanted. I* **said** *I would like some ice cream.*

## sail

**sails**
A **sail** is a large piece of cloth that is fixed to a boat. When the wind blows into the sail, it makes the boat move.

sail

## sail

**sails sailing sailed**
If you **sail** somewhere, you travel in a boat or a ship.

## sailor

**sailors**
A **sailor** is someone who is part of a ship's crew.

## salad

**salads**
A **salad** is a mixture of raw vegetables, such as lettuce and tomato.

## sale

**sales**
1 When a shop has a **sale**, it sells things for less than their usual price.
2 If something is **for sale**, people can buy it.

## salt

People use **salt** to give food flavour. You can add salt when you cook or you can shake it over your food.

## same

Things that are the **same** are just like each other. *Freddie's dogs look the* **same**.
■ *opposite* **different**

## sand

**Sand** is tiny pieces of rock and shell. Some beaches and deserts are covered with sand.

## sandal

**sandals**
A **sandal** is a light shoe with straps that go over your foot. People wear sandals when it is hot.

## sandwich

**sandwiches**
A **sandwich** is made from two pieces of bread with another food between them.
*Sam had cheese and salad sandwiches for lunch.*

## sang

**Sang** comes from the word **sing**.
*Aled often sings in concerts. He sang three songs last night.*

## sank

**Sank** comes from the word **sink**.
*The ship hit the rocks and began to sink. It sank to the bottom of the sea.*

## sari

**saris**
A **sari** is a long piece of light cloth that you wear wrapped round your body. Indian women and girls often wear saris.

## sat

**Sat** comes from the word **sit**.
*Jane could not find anywhere to sit. In the end, she sat on the floor.*

## satellite

**satellites**
**1** A **satellite** is a machine that travels around the Earth or another planet.

**2** A **satellite** is also a natural object that travels around a planet. The Moon is a satellite of the Earth.

## satellite dish

**satellite dishes**
A **satellite dish** is attached to a building to pick up TV signals from a satellite.

## satnav

**satnavs**
A **satnav** is a small computer that uses satellite signals to help drivers find their way. Satnav is short for satellite navigation.

## sauce

**sauces**
A **sauce** is a thick liquid that you eat with other food.

## saucepan

**saucepans**
A **saucepan** is a metal pot with a handle that is used for cooking.

a b c d e f g h i j k l m n o p q r s t u v w x y z

## sausage

**sausages**
A **sausage** is made from chopped meat inside a special skin.

## save

**saves saving saved**
1 If you **save** someone, you rescue them. *Lauren jumped into the water to **save** the child.*
2 If you **save** money, you keep it to use later. *Amelia is **saving** to buy some paints.*
3 If you **save** what you are doing on a computer, it is stored in the computer and you can look at it again later.

## saw

**saws**
A **saw** is a tool with a handle and a blade. You use a saw to cut wood.

## saw

**Saw** comes from the word **see**. *I see my cousin most weeks. I **saw** her twice last week.*

## say

**says saying said**
If you **say** something, you speak words. *Mark **said** "Hello" to me.*

## scale

**scales**
1 A **scale** is a set of musical notes that are played or sung in order.
2 A **scale** is also one of the small pieces of skin that cover the body of a fish or a reptile.

## scales

You use **scales** to find out how much something weighs. *Weigh the sugar on the **scales**.*

## scar

**scars**
A **scar** is a mark on your skin where a wound used to be.

## scare

**scares scaring scared**
If you **scare** someone, you make them feel frightened. *Jessica **scared** me with a toy spider.*

## scarf

**scarves**
A **scarf** is a piece of cloth that you wear round your neck. People wear scarves to keep warm.

## scatter

**scatters scattering scattered**
When you **scatter** things, you throw them over a large area.

*Tom scattered seeds for the birds to eat.*

## school

**schools**
A **school** is a place where children go to learn.

## science

When you study **science**, you find out about the Earth, space, people, animals or plants. You do experiments to help you learn about science.

## scientist

**scientists**
A **scientist** is someone who does experiments to find out more about the world.

## scissors

You use a pair of **scissors** to cut paper or cloth. Scissors have two handles and two blades.

## score

**scores**
A **score** is the number of points or goals that each side gets in a game. *What was the score in the football match?*

## score

**scores scoring scored**
When you **score** a goal, you make a ball go into a net.

*George scored three times in today's match.*

## scrap

**scraps**
A **scrap** is a small piece of something. *A scrap of paper. A scrap of food.*

## scrapbook

**scrapbooks**
A **scrapbook** is a book with plain pages. You stick pictures and photos in a scrapbook.

## scrape

**scrapes scraping scraped**
If you **scrape** something, you remove some of its surface by dragging something sharp across it. *Jacob scraped the potatoes with a knife. Amy scraped her knee on a rock.*

## scratch

**scratches scratching scratched**
1 If you **scratch** something, you make a small cut in it. *William scratched his arm in the bushes. Jo scratched her name with a pin.*
2 If you **scratch** yourself, you rub a part of you that itches.

## scream

**screams screaming screamed**
When you **scream**, you make a loud, high sound. People scream when they are very frightened, hurt or excited.

## screen

**screens**
A **screen** is a flat surface used for showing pictures. Computers and televisions have screens.

## screw

**screws**
A **screw** is a piece of pointed metal with a flat top. You twist screws into things to hold them together.

## scribble

**scribbles scribbling scribbled**
If you **scribble**, you write or draw quickly and carelessly. *Matt scribbled on the notepad.*

## scrub

**scrubs scrubbing scrubbed**
If you **scrub** something, you rub it hard to clean it. *Rosie scrubbed the carpet to get rid of the stains.*

## sea

**seas**
A **sea** is a very large area of salty water.

## sea creature

**sea creatures**
A **sea creature** is an animal that lives in the sea.

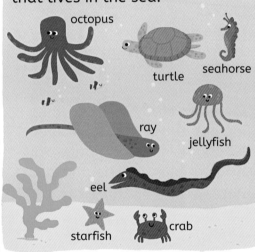

octopus
turtle
seahorse
ray
jellyfish
eel
starfish
crab

## seagull

**seagulls**
A **seagull** is a large bird that lives near the sea. Seagulls are usually grey and white.

## seal

**seals**

A **seal** is an animal with smooth fur that lives in the sea and on land. Seals eat fish and swim very well.

## seal

**seals sealing sealed**

When you **seal** something, you close it tightly. *Seal the envelope and put it in the post.*

## search

**searches searching searched**

If you **search** for something, you look for it. *We searched the house for our hamster, but we couldn't find it.*

## search engine

**search engines**

A **search engine** is a website that helps you find things on the internet.

## seaside

The **seaside** is a place by the sea where people go for their holidays. *We love going to the seaside because we can swim and play on the beach.*

## season

**seasons**

A **season** is a part of the year. The four seasons are spring, summer, autumn and winter.

## seat

**seats**

A **seat** is a place where you can sit. *There were only two seats left on the bus.*

## seaweed

**Seaweed** is a name for many types of plants that grow in the sea.

## second

**seconds**

A **second** is a very short amount of time. There are 60 seconds in a minute.

## secret

**secrets**

A **secret** is something that you keep hidden and do not tell people about. *We kept Cary's birthday present a secret.*

a b c d e f g h i j k l m n o p q r s t u v w x y z

## see

**sees seeing saw seen**
1 When you **see**, you notice things with your eyes.
2 When you **see** someone, you meet them. *I saw Daisy in town.*

## seed

**seeds**
A **seed** is a part of a plant. When you put seeds into the ground, new plants grow.

seed

## seem

**seems seeming seemed**
If something **seems** to be a particular way, that is the way it looks or feels. *The journey seemed longer than usual.*

## seen

**Seen** comes from the word **see**. *I want to see Vijay. I haven't seen him for weeks.*

> Some words with an "**s**" sound begin with "**ce**" or "**ci**", like **ceiling** or **city**.

## selfish

**Selfish** people think about themselves rather than others.

## sell

**sells selling sold**
Someone who **sells** things gives them to people for money.
■ *opposite* **buy**

## send

**sends sending sent**
If you **send** something, you make it go somewhere. *Josie sent a postcard to her auntie.*

Dear Auntie Floss,
We are having a great time in Naples. We went sailing and saw dolphins by our boat! And you won't believe all the ice cream flavours they have!
Love Josie

Mrs F. Fairbanks
26 Petticoat Lane
Tingleton, Shropshire
SY4 3RG ENGLAND

## sense

**senses**
1 Your **senses** help you to find out about the things around you. Your five senses are sight, hearing, touch, taste and smell.
2 If something **makes sense**, you can understand it.

## sensible

A **sensible** person thinks carefully and does not do stupid things.

## sent

**Sent** comes from the word **send**. *I must send a letter to Marc. He sent me two postcards last month.*

## sentence

**sentences**
A **sentence** is a group of words that makes sense. When you write down a sentence, you start with a capital letter and end with a full stop.

## separate

If things are **separate**, they are not joined together.

*Lewis put the bottles and tins in separate boxes.*

## series

A **series** is a group of things that follow each other. *A TV series.*

## serious

1  If something is **serious**, it is important and should be thought about carefully. *We must have a serious talk about your work.*
2  A **serious** person does not laugh and joke very much.

## serve

**serves serving served**
If someone **serves** you in a shop or a restaurant, they help you to buy what you want.

## set

**sets**
A **set** is a group of things that belong together. *A chess set.*

## set

**sets setting set**
1  When something is **set**, it is arranged or put in place. *Please set your watch to the right time.*
2  When the Sun **sets**, it goes out of sight in the evening.

## several

**Several** means a small number, usually more than three. *Dan has several pairs of jeans.*

## sew

**sews sewing sewed sewn**
▲ *rhymes with* **low**
When you **sew**, you join pieces of cloth together, using a needle and thread.

## sex

**sexes**
The **sexes** are the two groups that humans and animals are divided into. One sex is male and the other is female.

## shade

**Shade** is an area that is hidden from sunlight. *Lily sat in the shade because it was too hot.*

## shadow

**shadows**
A **shadow** is a dark shape made by something blocking out the light.

...... shadow

## shake

**shakes shaking shook shaken**
If you **shake** something, you move it up and down or from side to side quite hard. *Shake the bottle before you open it.*

## shall

**should**
1 **Shall** means will.
*I **shall** call you tomorrow.*
2 You also use **shall** to make suggestions.
*Shall we get ice cream?*

## shallow

**shallower shallowest**
Something that is **shallow** does not go down very far. *A **shallow** pool.*
■ opposite **deep**

## shampoo

**Shampoo** is a liquid that you use to wash your hair. You rub it into your hair and then rinse it out.

## shape

**shapes**
The **shape** of something is its outline, or the way it looks on the outside.

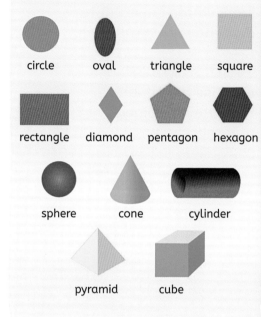

circle    oval    triangle    square

rectangle    diamond    pentagon    hexagon

sphere    cone    cylinder

pyramid    cube

## share

**shares sharing shared**
1 If you **share** something, you let others use it or have some of it. *Joe **shared** his photo online. Mary **shared** her sweets.*
2 **Share** also means to use something with other people. *I **share** the computer with my family.*

## shark

**sharks**
**Sharks** are big fish with sharp teeth. Sharks live in the sea.

184

## sharp

**sharper sharpest**
Something that is **sharp** has a very thin edge or a point that can cut or prick you. *A **sharp** knife. A **sharp** pencil.*
■ *opposite* **blunt**

## shave

**shaves shaving shaved**
When people **shave**, they cut hair from their skin. *Grandpa **shaves** every day.*

## she'd

1  **She'd** is a short way of saying **she had**. *She'd never been to Rome before.*
2  **She'd** is also a short way of saying **she would**. *Ask Zoe if **she'd** like some cake.*

## shed

**sheds**
A **shed** is a small, wooden building. People often keep tools in their sheds.

## sheep

**sheep**
A **sheep** is a farm animal with a woolly coat. Sheep are kept for their wool and their meat.

## sheet

**sheets**
1  A **sheet** is a large piece of cloth that you use to cover a mattress.
2  A **sheet** is also a flat piece of paper, glass or plastic.

## shelf

**shelves**
A **shelf** is a flat piece of wood, metal or plastic that is fixed to a wall. You keep things on shelves.

## she'll

**She'll** is a short way of saying **she will**. *Mel is finishing her lunch. **She'll** be here soon.*

## shell

**shells**
A **shell** is a hard cover around something. Eggs, nuts, snails and some sea creatures have shells.

**185**

a b c d e f g h i j k l m n o p q r s t u v w x y z

## shelter

**shelters**
A **shelter** is a place where you can stay dry and safe.

## she's

**1** **She's** is a short way of saying **she is**. *I'm waiting for Victoria to arrive. She's coming at 10 o'clock.*
**2** **She's** is also short for **she has**. *She's brought gifts for everyone.*

## shine

**shines shining shone**
If something **shines**, it gives off a bright light. *Hold the torch so that it shines on your face.*

## ship

**ships**
A **ship** is a large boat that carries people and things over the sea.

## shirt

**shirts**
A **shirt** is a piece of clothing that people wear on the top part of their bodies. Shirts often have a collar and fasten down the front.

## shiver

**shivers shivering shivered**
When you **shiver**, your body shakes because you are cold or frightened.

## shoe

**shoes**
▲ rhymes with **too**
A **shoe** is something that you wear to cover your foot. Shoes can be made of leather, plastic or cloth.

## shone

**Shone** comes from the word **shine**. *We hoped that the Sun would shine all day, but it only shone for a few hours.*

## shook

**Shook** comes from the word **shake**. *We told Andy to shake the orange juice, but he shook it too hard and the lid came off.*

## shoot

**shoots shooting shot**
**1** **Shoot** means to use a gun.
**2** When you **shoot** in a game such as football, you try to score a goal.

## shop

**shops**
A **shop** is a place where you can buy things.

## shore

**shores**
The **shore** is the land at the edge of a sea, lake or wide river. *We searched for shells along the shore.*

## short

**shorter shortest**
**1** If something is **short**, it is not very long. *Short hair. A short time.*
■ *opposite* **long**
**2** Someone who is **short** is not very tall.
■ *opposite* **tall**

## shorts

**Shorts** are short trousers. People wear shorts when it is hot or when they are playing sport.

## shot

**Shot** comes from the word **shoot**. *It's Danny's turn to shoot. Wayne has shot three times already in this match.*

## should

If you **should** do something, you ought to do it. *You should brush your teeth every day.*

## shoulder

**shoulders**
Your **shoulder** is the part of your body between your neck and your arm.

## shouldn't

**Shouldn't** is a short way of saying **should not**. *If you're that sick, you shouldn't go out at all.*

## shout

**shouts shouting shouted**
When you **shout**, you talk very loudly. *Jessie shouted to Nat to pass her the ball.*

## show

**shows**
A **show** is a performance that you usually see in a theatre. Shows often have music.

## show

**shows showing showed shown**
**1** If you **show** something, you let people see it. *Sophie showed everyone her new watch.*
**2** If you **show** someone how to do something, you do it and explain what you are doing. *Anna showed me how to knit.*

## shower

**showers**
1 A **shower** is a piece of equipment that sends out a spray of water. You wash yourself by standing under it.
2 A **shower** is also a short fall of rain.

## shown

**Shown** comes from the word **show**. *Asha wants to show her photographs to the class. She has already **shown** them to her family.*

## shrink

**shrinks shrinking shrank shrunk**
If something **shrinks**, it gets smaller. *My T-shirt **shrank** when it was washed.*

## shut

**shuts shutting shut**
1 If you **shut** a door, you move it so that it blocks a space in the wall.
2 If you **shut** a box, you put a lid on it.

## shut

If something is **shut**, people or things cannot go into it or through it. *The shop is **shut** on Sundays. The door was **shut** and locked.*

## shy

**shyer shyest**
If someone is **shy**, they are quiet and find it hard to talk to people they do not know.

## sick

1 If you feel **sick**, you do not feel well.
2 When you are **sick**, you bring up food from your stomach through your mouth.

*Kelly is feeling sick.*

## side

**sides**
1 A **side** is a surface of an object. *Use both **sides** of the paper. A cube has six **sides**.*
2 A **side** is also an edge. *Milly stayed at the **side** of the pool.*
3 A **side** is also a team. *Which **side** won the match?*

## sigh

**sighs sighing sighed**
When you **sigh**, you breathe out noisily. People usually sigh because they are sad or bored.

## sight

**sights**
1 A **sight** is something that you see. *A beautiful **sight**.*
2 **Sight** is the sense of seeing.

## sign

**signs**

1 A **sign** is a shape that means something. *The sign for a pound is £.*

2 A **sign** is also a set of words or pictures that tell you what to do or where to go.

*Picnic places are often marked with a **sign**.*

## sign

**signs signing signed**

When you **sign** something, you write your name on it.

## signal

**signals**

1 A **signal** is a message that does not use any words. *The climbers waved their arms as a signal to the rescue helicopter.*

2 An electrical **signal** carries information through the air. *A television signal.*

## silly

**sillier silliest**

If you are being **silly**, you are not behaving in a sensible way.

## silver

**Silver** is a shiny, grey metal that is valuable. Some jewellery and coins are made of silver.

## similar

If two things are **similar**, they are alike in some ways, but not exactly the same. *Leon and his brother look **similar**, but Leon has freckles.*

## simple

**simpler simplest**

If something is **simple**, it is very easy to do. *A simple sum.*

## since

1 **Since** means after. *I haven't seen Mandy since Friday.*

2 **Since** also means because. *Since you've been so good, you can stay up to watch the film.*

## sing

**sings singing sang sung**

When you **sing**, you use your voice to make music. *Toby loves singing along to the radio.*

## single

**Single** means only one. *There was a single rose in the vase.*

## sink

**sinks**

A **sink** is something that you wash things in. Sinks have taps and a plug. *Tom is washing the plates in the sink.*

## sink

**sinks sinking sank sunk**

If something **sinks**, it moves downwards, usually under water.

*Tim's shoe sank.*

## sip

**sips sipping sipped**

When you **sip** a drink, you drink a small amount at a time. *Becky sipped her hot chocolate.*

## sister

**sisters**

Your **sister** is a girl who has the same mum and dad as you.

## sit

**sits sitting sat**

When you **sit**, you rest your bottom on something. *We sat on the steps to wait for Jack.*

## size

**sizes**

The **size** of something is how big or small it is. *What size are your feet?*

## skate

**skates**

**Skates** are special boots that you wear to move smoothly on ice. Skates have a metal blade fixed to the bottom of them.

ice skate

## skate

**skates skating skated**

When you **skate**, you move along smoothly, wearing ice skates or roller skates.

## skateboard

**skateboards**

A **skateboard** is a narrow board with wheels fixed to the bottom of it. You ride a skateboard by standing on it and pushing off with one foot.

## skeleton

**skeletons**

A **skeleton** is all the bones in the body of a person or an animal.

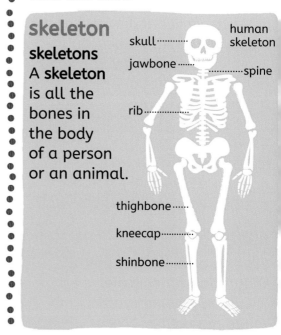

human skeleton

skull

jawbone

spine

rib

thighbone

kneecap

shinbone

## sketch
**sketches sketching sketched**
When you **sketch**, you make a quick drawing. *Lucy **sketched** her brothers while they were eating tea.*

## ski
**skis**
**Skis** are long, narrow strips of wood, metal or plastic. You fix skis to boots and use them to travel fast over snow.

## ski
**skis skiing skied**
When you **ski**, you travel fast over snow, wearing skis. *Jessica **skied** down the mountain.*

## skid
**skids skidding skidded**
If you **skid**, you slide on slippery ground. *Max **skidded** on the icy pavement.*

## skill
**skills**
If you have a **skill**, you are able to do something well. *Sarah's special **skill** is drawing.*

## skin
**skins**
**1** Your body is covered with **skin**. *Babies have very smooth **skin**.*
**2** The **skin** of a fruit or a vegetable is its outside layer.

banana skin

## skip
**skips skipping skipped**
**1** When you **skip**, you move by hopping first on one foot and then on the other.
**2** When you **skip** with a skipping rope, you keep swinging the rope over your head and jumping over it.

## skirt
**skirts**
A **skirt** is a piece of clothing worn by women and girls. Skirts hang from the waist.

## skull
**skulls**
Your **skull** is the bony part of your head. Your brain is inside your skull.

## sky
**skies**
The **sky** is the air that surrounds the Earth. On a sunny day, it is blue.

## slam

**slams slamming slammed**
When you **slam** a door, you shut it with a bang.

## slap

**slaps slapping slapped**
If you **slap** something, you hit it with the palm of your hand.

## sledge

**sledges**
A **sledge** is a small vehicle that you use to ride over snow.

## sleep

**sleeps sleeping slept**
When you **sleep**, you close your eyes and rest your whole body. Most people sleep at night.

## sleet

**Sleet** is icy rain. It looks like wet snow.

## sleeve

**sleeves**
A **sleeve** is the part of a piece of clothing that covers your arm. *This shirt has long sleeves.*

## sleigh

**sleighs**
A **sleigh** is a sledge that is pulled by a horse or a reindeer.

## slept

**Slept** comes from the word **sleep**. *Anna doesn't usually sleep well, but she slept for hours last night.*

## slice

**slices**
A **slice** is a piece of food that has been cut from a larger piece. *A slice of cake.*

## slide

**slides**
A **slide** is something that you play on in playgrounds. You climb up steps and then slide down.

## slide

**slides sliding slid**
When something **slides**, it moves smoothly over something else. *Leah slid the book across the table.*

# slimy

**slimier slimiest**
Something that is **slimy** is slippery and sticky.
*Slimy green goo.*

# slip

**slips slipping slipped**
If you **slip**, you slide by accident and often fall over.

*Jacob slipped on the wet floor.*

# slipper

**slippers**
A **slipper** is a soft, comfortable shoe that you wear indoors.

# slippery

If something is **slippery**, it is difficult to grip or to walk on.

# slope

**slopes sloping sloped**
If something **slopes**, it is higher at one end than the other. *The lawn **slopes** down to the gate.*

# slot

**slots**
A **slot** is a small, narrow space that you put something in.
*Put a coin in the slot.*

# slow

**slower slowest**
Something that is **slow** takes a long time to go somewhere or to do something. *A **slow** train.*
■ *opposite* **fast**

# slug

**slugs**
A **slug** is a slimy little animal with no legs and a soft body.

# smack

**smacks smacking smacked**
If you **smack** someone, you hit them with the palm of your hand.

# small

**smaller smallest**
Something that is **small** is little.
■ *opposite* **big**

Some other words for **small** are **little**, **tiny** and **titchy**.

# smartphone

**smartphones**
A **smartphone** is a mobile phone that has apps, and that can use the internet.

a b c d e f g h i j k l m n o p q r s t u v w x y z

## smash

**smashes smashing smashed**
If something **smashes**, it breaks into lots of pieces because it has been dropped or hit. *The cup smashed when Robert dropped it.*

## smell

**smells smelling smelt**
1 When you **smell** something, you find out about it by using your nose. *Kate smelt the flowers.*
2 If something **smells**, you notice it by using your nose. *That cake smells good.*

## smile

**smiles smiling smiled**
When you **smile**, the corners of your mouth turn up. You smile when you are happy or when you think that something is funny.

## smoke

**Smoke** is made when something burns. Smoke usually looks like a white or grey cloud.

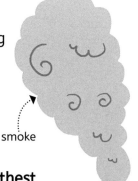

smoke

## smooth

**smoother smoothest**
Something that is **smooth** does not have any bumps or lumps in it. *Smooth skin. A smooth sauce.*

## snack

**snacks**
A **snack** is a small meal that you can eat quickly. *We had a snack when we got home from school.*

## snail

**snails**
A **snail** is a small animal with no legs and a soft body. Snails have shells on their backs.

## snake

**snakes**
A **snake** is a long, thin reptile with no legs. Snakes move by sliding their bodies along the ground. Some snakes have poisonous bites.

## snap

**snaps snapping snapped**
When something **snaps**, it breaks with a sudden noise. *The twig snapped when Tom bent it.*

# snatch

**snatches snatching snatched**
If you **snatch** something, you take it quickly and roughly. *Benjamin **snatched** the letter out of my hands.*

# sneeze

**sneezes sneezing sneezed**
When you **sneeze**, air rushes out of your nose and mouth with a loud noise. You often sneeze when you have a cold.

# sniff

**sniffs sniffing sniffed**
When you **sniff**, you breathe in hard through your nose.

*Jemimah **sniffed** the flower.*

# snore

**snores snoring snored**
If you **snore**, you breathe noisily through your mouth while you are asleep.

# snow

**snows snowing snowed**
When it **snows**, soft, white pieces of ice, called snowflakes, fall from the sky.

# soak

**soaks soaking soaked**
When water **soaks** into something, it makes it very wet. *The rain has **soaked** my trousers.*

# soap

**soaps**
You mix **soap** with water to wash and clean things.

# sock

**socks**
**Socks** are clothes that you wear on your feet, inside your shoes.

*A pair of **socks**.*

# sofa

**sofas**
A **sofa** is a long, comfortable seat for two or more people.

# soft

**softer softest**
1 If something is **soft**, it is not hard or firm. Soft things change shape easily. *A **soft** pillow.*
■ opposite **hard**
2 **Soft** also means quiet and gentle. *A **soft** voice.*

# soil

**Soil** is the ground that plants grow in.

a b c d e f g h i j k l m n o p q r s t u v w x y z

## sold

**Sold** comes from the word **sell**. *Jasmine decided to sell her books. She had soon **sold** them all.*

## soldier

**soldiers**
A **soldier** is a member of an army.

## solid

Something that is **solid** does not change shape easily. Wood and metal are solid.

## some

**Some** means an amount. *We had **some** soup for lunch.*

## somebody

**Somebody** means a person. *Can **somebody** help me, please?*

## someone

**Someone** means a person. *I saw **someone** that looked like you.*

## somersault

**somersaults**
When you do a **somersault**, you roll over forwards so that your feet go over your head. You can do somersaults on the ground or in the air.

## something

**Something** means a thing. *I want to show you **something** amazing.*

## sometimes

**Sometimes** means at some times. *We **sometimes** hear the dog next door howling.*

## somewhere

**Somewhere** means a place. *I put my book down **somewhere**.*

## son

**sons**
A **son** is someone's male child.

## song

**songs**
A **song** is a piece of music with words that you sing.

## soon

**sooner soonest**
If something will happen **soon**, it will begin in a short time. *It will **soon** be bedtime.*

## sore

**sorer sorest**
If part of your body is **sore**, it hurts. *A **sore** knee.*

## sorry

1  If you feel **sorry** about something, you feel sad about it. *I am **sorry** that you are not well.*
2  You say **sorry** when you are upset that you have done something wrong.

## sort

**sorts**
Things of the same **sort** belong to the same group. *What sort of dog do you like best?*

## sound

**sounds**
A **sound** is something that you hear. *Bees make a buzzing sound.*

## soup

**soups**
**Soup** is a liquid food that you usually eat hot. Soup is made from meat or vegetables and water.

## sour

If something is **sour**, it has a taste like lemons or vinegar. *These apples are really sour!*

## south

**South** is a direction. If you face the Sun when it rises, south is on your right.
■ *opposite* **north**

## sow

**sows sowing sowed sown**
▲ *rhymes with* **low**
When you **sow** seeds, you put them in soil so that they can grow.

## space

**spaces**
1  A **space** is an empty place or area. *We found a space to park the car.*
2  **Space** is the area outside the Earth. The stars and planets are in space.

## spacecraft

**spacecraft**
A **spacecraft** is a vehicle that travels into space. Spacecraft carry astronauts and their equipment.

## spade

**spades**
A **spade** is a tool that you use to dig. A spade has a long handle and a flat metal end.

a b c d e f g h i j k l m n o p q r s t u v w x y z

## spare

**Spare** means left over. *What do you do in your **spare** time?*

## speak

**speaks speaking spoke spoken**
When you **speak**, you use your voice to make words. *Henry **speaks** loudly.*

## special

1 If something is **special**, it is important or better than usual. *A **special** meal.*
2 Something that is **special** is made to do a particular job. *You need to take **special** equipment when you go camping.*

## speed

The **speed** of something is how fast it moves. *Cheetahs run at an amazing **speed**.*

## spell

**spells spelling spelt**
When you **spell** a word, you write or say its letters in the right order. *Can you **spell** my name?*

## spend

**spends spending spent**
1 When you **spend** money, you use it to buy things. *Izzy **spent** all her pocket money on sweets.*
2 If you **spend** time doing something, you use that time to do it. *I **spent** half an hour practising the piano.*

## spider

**spiders**
A **spider** is an animal with eight legs. Spiders make webs to catch insects.

## spike

**spikes**
A **spike** is a sharp point.

## spill

**spills spilling spilt**
If you **spill** a liquid, you let it fall out of its container by accident. *Joel has **spilt** the milk.*

## spin

**spins spinning spun**
When something **spins**, it keeps turning round quickly. *Eleanor started **spinning** the top as fast as she could.*

## splash

**splashes splashing splashed**
When someone **splashes**, they throw water around. *Sarah **splashed** in the waves.*

## split

**splits splitting split**
If something **splits**, it tears or comes apart. *Ryan's shirt has **split** down the side.*

## spoil

**spoils spoiling spoilt**
If you **spoil** something, you damage it or make it worse. *Amy spoilt the soup by adding too much salt.*

## spoilt

**Spoilt** children have too many things and are allowed to do what they like too often.

## spoke

**Spoke** comes from the word **speak**. *Aidan usually speaks very quietly, but he spoke loudly to the class.*

## sponge

**sponges**
**Sponge** is a soft material with lots of holes in it. Sponges can soak up water and are used for cleaning and for washing yourself.

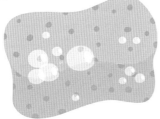

## spoon

**spoons**
You use a **spoon** to stir things and to eat with. Spoons have a handle and a rounded end for holding food.

## sport

**sports**
A **sport** is a kind of game that you do to exercise. Football and tennis are sports.

## spot

**spots**
1 A **spot** is a round mark or shape. *Lara's dress has yellow spots on it.*
2 A **spot** is also a small lump on your skin.

## spot

**spots spotting spotted**
If you **spot** something, you notice it with your eyes. *Jack spotted some toadstools in the wood.*

## spout

**spouts**
A **spout** is a kind of tube on a kettle or a teapot. You pour liquid out of a spout.

## spray

**Spray** is lots of tiny drops of water or other liquid. *The waves crashed against the rocks and covered us in spray.*

A
B
C
D
E
F
G
H
I
J
K
L
M
N
O
P
Q
R
S
T
U
V
W
X
Y
Z

## spread

**spreads spreading spread**
**1** If you **spread** something **out**, you lay or stretch it out over a surface. *Nella* **spread** *the map* **out** *on the table.*
**2** If you **spread** something soft, you put a layer of it on something else. ***Spread*** *some butter on your bread.*
**3** When you **spread** some news, you tell lots of people about it.

## spring

**springs**
**1** A **spring** is a piece of wire that is wound into circles. Springs jump back into shape when you press them.
**2** **Spring** is also one of the four seasons. It comes between winter and summer. In the spring, the weather gets warmer and plants begin to grow.

## spun

**Spun** comes from the word **spin**. *The skater began to spin around. She* **spun** *seven times.*

## spy

**spies**
A **spy** is someone who secretly watches other people to get information.

## square

**squares**
A **square** is a shape with four corners, and four sides of equal length.

## squash

**squashes squashing squashed**
If you **squash** something, you press it and make it flatter. *Nat stood on a tomato and* **squashed** *it.*

## squeal

**squeals squealing squealed**
When you **squeal**, you make a long, high sound because you are excited or frightened.

## squeeze

**squeezes squeezing squeezed**
When you **squeeze** something, you press its sides together. *Malik* **squeezed** *the toothpaste tube.*

## squirrel

**squirrels**
A **squirrel** is a small animal with a big, furry tail. Squirrels live in trees and are very good at climbing.

## stable

**stables**
A **stable** is a building where horses are kept.

## stack

**stacks stacking stacked**
If you **stack** things, you put them one on top of another. *Oliver stacked his comics on the table.*

## stage

**stages**
A **stage** is an area in a theatre or a hall where plays and concerts are performed.

## stain

**stains**
A **stain** is a mark that is hard to remove.

## stairs

**Stairs** are a set of steps that you use to walk up and down, usually inside a building.

## stalk

**stalks**
A **stalk** is the long, central part of a plant. Leaves, flowers and fruit grow from the stalk. Stalk is another word for **stem**.

## stamp

**stamps**
A **stamp** is a small piece of paper with a picture printed on it. You stick stamps on letters and parcels to show that you have paid to post them.

## stamp

**stamps stamping stamped**
If you **stamp** your foot, you put it down hard on the ground.

## stand

**stands standing stood**
When you **stand**, you are on your feet and upright. *Stand up straight!*

## stank

**Stank** comes from the word **stink**. *My brother's feet stink. After his run, they stank even more than usual.*

## star

**stars**
1 A **star** is a huge ball of burning gases in space. At night, stars look like tiny points of light in the sky.
2 A **star** is also a shape with points.
3 A **star** is also a famous person, such as an actor or a singer.

## stare

**stares staring stared**
If you **stare** at something, you look at it for a long time with your eyes wide open.

## start

**starts starting started**
When you **start** to do something, you do the first part of it. *Maria started to tidy her room.*

## starve

**starves starving starved**
If someone **starves**, they become very ill or die because they do not have enough to eat.

## station

**stations**
1 A **station** is a place where trains stop.
2 A **station** is also a building where police or firefighters work.
3 A **station** is also a company that provides television or radio programmes.

## statue

**statues**
A **statue** is a large model of a person or an animal. Statues are made from stone, metal or some other hard material.

Statue of Liberty

## stay

**stays staying stayed**
1 If you **stay** in a place, you do not leave it. *We stayed at home all day.*
2 If you **stay** with someone, you live with them for a short time. *We are staying with my uncle for a week.*

## steady

**steadier steadiest**
If something is **steady**, it does not move about or shake. *You need a steady hand to hold the camera still.*

## steal

**steals stealing stole stolen**
People who **steal** take things that do not belong to them.

## steam

**Steam** is water that has boiled and turned into a cloud of tiny water drops.

## steel

**Steel** is a hard, strong metal that is made mostly from iron.

## steep

**steeper steepest**
Something that
is **steep**
slopes
a lot.

*Natalie
climbed
the **steep**
hill.*

## steer

**steers steering steered**
When you **steer** a bicycle or
a car, you make it go in
the direction you want.

## stem

**stems**
A **stem** is the
long, central
part of a
plant.

stem

## step

**steps**
1  When you take a **step**,
you move your foot forward
and then put it down.
2  A **step** is a flat surface
that you put your foot on
when you climb up or down.
*There are three **steps**
outside our front door.*

## stick

**sticks**
A **stick** is a long, thin piece
of wood.

## stick

**sticks sticking stuck**
1  If you **stick** two things
together, you use glue
to join them.
2  If you **stick** a pin or a needle
into something, you push it in.
*Susannah **stuck** a needle into
her finger by accident.*

## sticker

**stickers**
A **sticker** is a sticky piece of
paper with pictures or writing
on it. *Lucy has stuck animal
**stickers** all over her
bedroom door.*

## sticky

**stickier stickiest**
If something is **sticky**, it
sticks to things.

## stiff

**stiffer stiffest**
Something that is **stiff** is hard
to bend or move. *The handle
was **stiff**. **Stiff** cardboard.*

# stile

**stiles**
A **stile** is a kind of step that you use to climb over a wall or a fence. Stiles are made of wood or stone.

# still

**1** Something that is **still** is not moving. *Everything was still and silent.*
**2** If something is **still** happening, it has not stopped. *Maggie was still asleep when Lisa arrived.*

# sting

**stings stinging stung**
If an insect **stings** you, it pricks your skin and leaves some poison in your body.

# stink

**stinks stinking stank stunk**
If something **stinks**, it smells horrible. *This cheese stinks!*

# stir

**stirs stirring stirred**
If you **stir** a liquid or a mixture, you move it around with a spoon or a stick. *Louie stirred all the ingredients together in a bowl.*

# stitch

**stitches**
A **stitch** is a loop of thread on a piece of cloth. You use a needle and thread to make stitches.

# stole

**Stole** comes from the word **steal**. *Mum told us never to steal. Dan stole a pencil and she was cross.*

# stomach

**stomachs**
▲ *say stum-uck*
Your **stomach** is the part of your body where your food goes after you have eaten it.

# stone

**stones**
**1** **Stone** is very hard and is found under the ground. Stone is used for building.
**2** A **stone** is a small piece of rock that you find on the ground.
**3** A **stone** is also the hard seed in the middle of fruits such as plums or peaches.

# stood

**Stood** comes from the word **stand**. *We had to stand in a queue for the cinema. We stood there for half an hour.*

# stool

**stools**
A **stool** is a seat without a back.

## stop

**stops stopping stopped**
**1** If something **stops**, it no longer happens. *It has **stopped** snowing.*
**2** When something **stops**, it no longer moves. *The bus **stopped**.*

## store

**stores storing stored**
When you **store** things, you put them away until you need them. *James **stores** his toys in a chest.*

## storm

**storms**
When there is a **storm**, it rains hard and the wind blows very strongly. Sometimes there is also thunder and lightning.

## story

**stories**
A **story** tells you about something that has happened. Stories can be true or made up.

## straight

**straighter straightest**
Something that is **straight** does not bend or curve. *Use a ruler to draw a **straight** line.*
■ *opposite* **bent**

## strange

**stranger strangest**
**Strange** things are unusual, or are different from what you expect. *A **strange** dream.*

## stranger

**strangers**
A **stranger** is someone you do not know.

## strap

**straps**
A **strap** is a strip of leather or other material. Straps are often used to hold things together.

## straw

**straws**
**1** **Straw** is the name for dry stalks of plants, such as corn and wheat. Farm animals often sleep on straw.
**2** A **straw** is a thin plastic tube that you use to suck drink into your mouth.

## strawberry

**strawberries**
A **strawberry** is a soft, red fruit with tiny, yellow seeds on its skin.

## stream

**streams**
A **stream** is a small river.

205

## street

**streets**

A **street** is a road. Streets usually have buildings on both sides.

## strength

The **strength** of something is how strong it is.

## stretch

**stretches stretching stretched**

**1** If you **stretch** something, you make it longer or bigger. *Simon stretched the rubber band until it snapped.*
**2** When you **stretch**, you push your arms up or out as far as they will go.

*Miriam stretched up high.*

## stretcher

**stretchers**

A **stretcher** is a narrow bed that is used to carry someone who is hurt or ill.

## strict

**stricter strictest**

A **strict** person makes you behave and do what you are told. *Our teacher is very strict.*

## strike

**strikes striking struck**

**1** If you **strike** something, you hit it.
**2** When you **strike** a match, you light it.
**3** When a clock **strikes**, it makes a sound to tell you what time it is. *The clock strikes every hour.*

## string

**strings**

**1** **String** is thin rope. People use string to tie things together.
**2** Some musical instruments have **strings**. You pluck the strings or rub them with a bow to make notes.

harp strings ·····

## strip

**strips**

A **strip** is a narrow piece of something, like paper or material.

## stripe

**stripes**

A **stripe** is a line of colour. *Ali's shirt has red and white stripes on it.*

# stroke

**strokes stroking stroked**
When you **stroke** an animal, you move your hand over it gently. *Rachel **stroked** the cat.*

# strong

**stronger strongest**
**1** A **strong** person can lift heavy things and has a lot of energy. *Keith is very **strong**.*
**2** Something **strong** does not break easily. *A **strong** box.*
■ *opposite* **weak**

# struck

**Struck** comes from the word **strike**. *Our clock strikes every hour. It has just **struck** seven.*

# struggle

**struggles struggling struggled**
If you **struggle**, you find something difficult to do. *Bill is **struggling** with his homework.*

# stuck

**Stuck** comes from the word **stick**. If you are **stuck**, you can't move or carry on. *The cat got **stuck** in the hole. My dad helped me with my homework because I was **stuck**.*

# student

**students**
A **student** is someone who is learning something, usually at school or college.

# study

**studies studying studied**
When you **study** something, you learn about it.

# stuff

**Stuff** means things or possessions. *There's so much **stuff** to do. Lily took all my **stuff**.*

# stuff

**stuffs stuffing stuffed**
If you **stuff** something into a bag, you push it in roughly.

# stung

**Stung** comes from the word **sting**. *Chloe is scared that the bee might sting her. She has been **stung** twice before.*

# stupid

**stupider stupidest**
If you are being **stupid**, you do silly things and are not sensible.

# subject

**subjects**
A **subject** is something that you learn about. Science and art are subjects.

## submarine

**submarines**

A **submarine** is a ship that can travel under water.

## subtract

**subtracts subtracting subtracted**

When you **subtract**, you take one number away from another. *Hannah **subtracted** seven from twelve.*

$$12-7=5$$

■ opposite **add**

## successful

Someone who is **successful** has done well at something. *A **successful** writer.*

## suck

**sucks sucking sucked**

1 When you **suck**, you pull in liquid through your mouth. *Alice **sucked** her juice through a straw.*

2 If you **suck** a sweet, you roll it around in your mouth without chewing it.

## sudden

Something **sudden** happens very quickly and is not expected. *We heard a **sudden** shout.*

## sugar

You put **sugar** in food or drink to make it taste sweet. Sugar grains are white or brown.

## suggest

**suggests suggesting suggested**

If you **suggest** something, you give someone an idea that might help them. *Holly **suggested** that we should try the other path.*

## suit

**suits**

A **suit** is a set of clothes that are meant to be worn together. Suits are made up of a jacket and trousers or a jacket and a skirt.

## suitable

Something that is **suitable** is right for a particular job. *Wear **suitable** clothes for painting.*

## suitcase

**suitcases**

You use a **suitcase** to carry your clothes when you travel.

## sum

**sums**

A **sum** is a maths question. *I have some **sums** for homework.*

# summer

**Summer** is one of the four seasons. It comes between spring and autumn. Summer is the warmest season.

# Sun

The **Sun** is the very big, bright light that you see in the sky in the daytime. It gives us heat and light. The Earth takes a year to go round the Sun.

# sunflower

**sunflowers**
A **sunflower** is a very tall flower with a large centre and yellow petals.

*Giant sunflowers are taller than grown-ups.*

# sung

**Sung** comes from the word **sing**. *Maria loves to sing. She has* **sung** *in several concerts.*

# sunk

**Sunk** comes from the word **sink**. *Some things float and others sink. The stone has* **sunk** *to the bottom of the bucket.*

# sunlight

**Sunlight** is the light that comes from the Sun. Most plants need sunlight to grow.

# sunny

**sunnier**
**sunniest**
When it is **sunny**, the Sun is shining.

# sunshine

**Sunshine** is the light and warmth that comes from the Sun. *Go out and play in the* **sunshine**!

# supermarket

**supermarkets**
A **supermarket** is a large shop that sells food and other things that you need at home.

# supper

**suppers**
**Supper** is a meal or a snack that you eat in the evening.

# support

**supports supporting supported**
1  If you **support** something, you hold it so that it does not fall. *Support the baby's head when you hold her.*
2  When you **support** people, you help them. *We* **supported** *Carly when she got into trouble.*
3  When you **support** a team, you want them to win.

a b c d e f g h i j k l m n o p q r s t u v w x y z

## suppose

**supposes supposing supposed**
**1** If you **suppose** something will happen, you expect that it will. *I suppose Justin will be late.*
**2** If you are **supposed to** do something, you are meant to do it. *I'm supposed to make my bed every morning.*

## sure

▲ say **shore**
If you are **sure** about something, you know that it is right. *Alistair was sure that he had seen the film before.*

## surface

**surfaces**
A **surface** is the outer part, or top of something. *The surface of the table is very scratched.*

## surname

**surnames**
Your **surname** is your last name or your family name.

## surprise

**surprises**
A **surprise** is something that you do not expect. *The party was a surprise.*

## surround

**surrounds surrounding surrounded**
If something **surrounds** you, it is all around you. *The juggler was surrounded by a crowd.*

## swallow

**swallows swallowing swallowed**
When you **swallow** food, it goes down your throat into your stomach.

## swam

**Swam** comes from the word **swim**. *Katherine tries to swim as often as she can. She swam every day last week.*

## swan

**swans**
A **swan** is a large, white bird with a long neck. Swans swim on rivers and lakes.

## swap

**swaps swapping swapped**
▲ rhymes with **top**
If you **swap** with someone, you give them something of yours and they give you something of theirs. *Jack and Jill swapped comics.*

## sway

**sways swaying swayed**
If you **sway**, you move slowly from side to side. *Tamsin swayed to the music.*

# swear

**swears swearing swore sworn**
**1** If you **swear**, you use
rude words.
**2** If you **swear** to do something,
you promise to do it. *Leo made*
*Rick swear to keep silent.*

# sweat

**sweats sweating sweated**
When you **sweat**, water comes
out of tiny holes in your skin.
You sweat when you are hot
or nervous.

# sweater

**sweaters**
A **sweater** is a knitted piece of
clothing that covers the top
part of your body.
Sweaters are often
made from wool
and are worn over
other clothes.

# sweet

**sweets**
A **sweet** is a small type of food
that tastes sweet. *James has*
*chosen all his favourite sweets.*

# sweet

**sweeter sweetest**
**1** Food that is **sweet** tastes
as though it has sugar in it.
**2** If something is **sweet**, it is
lovely. *A sweet kitten.*
**3** If someone is **sweet**, they
are kind. *It was sweet of Emily*
*to give me a present.*

# swim

**swims swimming swam swum**
When you **swim**, you move
through water using your
arms and legs.

*Milo swims*
*every day.*

# swing

**swings**
A **swing** is
a seat that
hangs from
ropes or chains.
You sit on a swing
and make it move
backwards and
forwards.
*We have a*
*swing hanging*
*from our*
*apple tree.*

# swing

**swings swinging swung**
If something **swings**, it moves
backwards and forwards while
hanging from something.

# switch

**switches**
You turn or press a **switch** to
make something electrical start
or stop. *A light switch.*

## swollen

Something that is **swollen** is larger than usual. *Pete has a swollen ankle.*

## sword

**swords**

▲ say **sord**

A **sword** is a weapon with a handle and a long, sharp blade. In the past, soldiers fought with swords. *A toy sword.*

## swore

**Swore** comes from the word **swear**. *Sam made me swear to keep his secret. I swore not to tell anyone.*

## swum

**Swum** comes from the word **swim**. *I always swim on holiday. I have swum every day so far.*

## swung

**Swung** comes from the word **swing**. *Elsa started to swing from the tree. She swung higher and higher each time.*

## syrup

**Syrup** is a thick, sweet liquid that is made from sugar. *Paul bought some syrup to make flapjacks.*

## table

**tables**

A **table** is a piece of furniture with legs and a flat top.

## tablet

**tablets**

1  A **tablet** is a small, dry piece of medicine. People swallow tablets when they are ill to make them feel better again.
2  A **tablet** is also a small, light computer with a touch screen.

## tadpole

**tadpoles**

A **tadpole** is a small creature that will grow into a frog or a toad. Tadpoles hatch from eggs and live in water.

## tail

**tails**

A **tail** is the part at the end of an animal's body.

# take

**takes taking took taken**
**1 Take** means to remove something or steal something. *Keith has **taken** my pen.*
**2 Take** also means to bring something with you. *Don't forget to **take** your umbrella.*
**3** If something **takes** an amount of time, that is how long it goes on for. *The journey **took** an hour.*

# takeaway

**takeaways**
A **takeaway** is a meal that you buy and take away to eat somewhere else.

# tale

**tales**
A **tale** is a story. *A fairy **tale**.*

# talent

**talents**
If you have a **talent** for something, you can do it very well. *Craig has a **talent** for drawing.*

# talk

**talks talking talked**
When you **talk**, you speak to people.

# tall

**taller tallest**
If something is **tall**, the top of it is high above the ground. *A **tall** tower.*
■ *opposite* **short**

# tame

**tamer tamest**
A **tame** animal is not wild and will not hurt people. Tame animals can be kept as pets.
■ *opposite* **wild**

# tangerine

**tangerines**
A **tangerine** is a small, sweet orange that you can peel easily.

# tangle

**tangles**
A **tangle** is a bunch of knots that has been made by accident.

*The wool is full of **tangles**.*

# tank

**tanks**
**1** A **tank** is a large container for liquids. *A water **tank**.*
**2** A **tank** is also a large, heavy vehicle with a gun. Tanks are used by soldiers.

# tap

**taps**
A **tap** is something that you turn to make water run or stop. Sinks and baths have taps.

## tap

**taps tapping tapped**
If you **tap** something, you hit it gently. *Jonathan **tapped** the table with his fingers.*

## tape

**Tape** is a long, thin strip of paper, cloth or plastic. *Sticky **tape**.*

## tape measure

**tape measures**
A **tape measure** is a long, thin strip, marked with centimetres or inches. You use a tape measure to measure things.

## target

**targets**
A **target** is something that people aim at. *Robin aimed his arrow at the centre of the **target**.*

## tart

**tarts**
A **tart** is a pie with no pastry on top. *A strawberry **tart**.*

## taste

**tastes tasting tasted**
When you **taste** food or drink, you put it in your mouth to find out what it is like. *Leo **tasted** the soup to see if he liked it.*

## tasty

**tastier tastiest**
Food that is **tasty** has a lovely flavour. *A **tasty** pie.*

## taught

**Taught** comes from the word **teach**. *My dad teaches people to swim. He **taught** me when I was small.*

## taxi

**taxis**
A **taxi** is a car that you pay to ride in. *We took a **taxi** to the station.*

## tea

**teas**
1  **Tea** is a drink. People make tea by pouring boiling water onto the chopped, dried leaves of the tea plant.
2  **Tea** is a meal that you eat in the afternoon or the early evening.

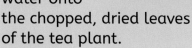

## teabag

**teabags**
A **teabag** is a small bag of chopped, dried leaves from the tea plant. People pour boiling water onto teabags to make tea.

# teach

**teaches teaching taught**
When people **teach** you something, they help you to understand it, or they show you how to do it. *Monica is teaching me how to play the piano.*

# teacher

**teachers**
A **teacher** is someone whose job is to teach other people. Teachers usually work in schools. *Mrs Parsnip is our class teacher.*

# team

**teams**
A **team** is a group of people who work together or play a sport together. *Alex plays in the school football team.*

# teapot

**teapots**
A **teapot** is a container that people use to make and pour tea. A teapot has a handle, a lid and a spout.

spout

handle

# tear

**tears**
▲ *rhymes with* **deer**
**Tears** are drops of water that come from your eyes when you cry. *Tears poured down her face.*

# tear

**tear tearing tore torn**
▲ *rhymes with* **bare**
When you **tear** something, you pull one part of it away from the rest. *Fraser tore his shirt on a nail.*

# tease

**teases teasing teased**
If you **tease** someone, you make jokes about them, either in a playful way, or in a cruel way.

# teddy bear

**teddy bears**
A **teddy bear** is a soft, furry toy that looks like a bear.

# teenager

**teenagers**
A **teenager** is someone who is between 13 and 19 years old.

# telephone

**telephones**
A **telephone** is a machine that you use to speak to someone in another place.

215

## telescope

**telescopes**
A **telescope** makes things that are far away look larger and closer. People use telescopes to look at the stars.

## television

**televisions**
A **television** is a machine that shows pictures and sends out sounds. Televisions receive signals through the air and turn them into pictures and sounds. TV is short for television.

## tell

**tells telling told**
1  If you **tell** someone something, you let them know about it. *Laura **told** me about her holiday.*
2  When someone **tells** you **to** do something, they say that you must do it. *Mum **told** me **to** go to bed.*
3  If you **can tell** something, you know it without being told. *I **can tell** that Sam is sad.*

## temperature

**temperatures**
The **temperature** of something is how hot or cold it is.

## tennis

**Tennis** is a game played by two or four players with rackets and a ball. The players hit the ball to each other over a net.

## tent

**tents**
A **tent** is a shelter made of strong material and held up by poles and ropes. You sleep in a tent when you go camping.

## term

**terms**
A **term** is one part of the school year. There are usually three terms in a year.

## terrible

If something is **terrible**, it is very bad. *A **terrible** film.*

## test

**tests**
You take a **test** to show how much you know about something. *A maths **test**.*

## test
**tests testing tested**
When you **test** something, you try it to see if it works properly. *Ella **tested** the new recipe.*

## text
**texts**
A **text** is a message that you can send from one mobile phone to another.

## thank
**thanks thanking thanked**
When you **thank** someone, you tell them you are pleased about something they have done. *I **thanked** Jay for helping me.*

## that's
1 **That's** is a short way of saying **that is**. *Evie, **that's** a lovely dress.*
2 **That's** is also a short way of saying **that has**. ***That's** been bothering me all day.*

## theatre
**theatres**
A **theatre** is a building where you go to see plays or shows.

## their
**Their** means belonging to them. *Do all the children have **their** tickets with them?*

## them
You use **them** to mean more than one person or thing. *I baked two cakes yesterday. Today I will decorate **them**.*

## themselves
**Themselves** means them and no one else. *The children dressed **themselves**.*

## then
1 **Then** means afterwards. *Eat your tea, **then** you can go out.*
2 **Then** also means at that time. *I did this painting last year. I wasn't as good **then** as I am now.*

## there
1 **There** means to or at that place. *Have you been **there** before? Put them down **there**.*
■ opposite **here**
2 You also use the word **there** to make someone notice something. ***There** is a cat in the tree.*

## there's

**1** **There's** is a short way of saying **there is**. *There's lots of food left.*
**2** **There's** is also a short way of saying **there has**. *There's been an accident.*

## thermometer

**thermometers**
You use a **thermometer** to find out how hot or cold something is. *We hung a thermometer in the garden and looked at it every day.*

## they

You use the word **they** when you talk about more than one person. *Rosa and Robin are best friends. They go everywhere together.*

## they'd

**1** **They'd** is a short way of saying **they had**. *The boys were late because they'd lost their way.*
**2** **They'd** is also a short way of saying **they would**. *The girls promised they'd return.*

## they'll

**They'll** is a short way of saying **they will**. *The boys have said that they'll be here soon.*

## they're

**They're** is a short way of saying **they are**. *The girls are very excited because they're going on holiday.*

## they've

**They've** is a short way of saying **they have**. *The Robinsons are away. They've gone on holiday for a week.*

## thick

**thicker thickest**
**1** If something is **thick**, it is deep or wide. *A thick book.*
**2** A **thick** liquid does not pour easily.
■ opposite **thin**

*Lydia loves thick syrup.*

## thief

**thieves**
**Thieves** take things that do not belong to them.

## thigh

**thighs**
Your **thigh** is the part of your leg between your knee and your hip.

# thin

**thinner thinnest**
1 If something is **thin**, it is narrow. *A **thin** belt.*
■ *opposite* **thick**
2 **Thin** people are not fat and do not weigh very much.
■ *opposite* **fat**

# thing

**things**
A **thing** is an object or an action. *Take your **things** off the table. There are lots of **things** to do.*

# think

**thinks thinking thought**
1 When you **think**, you use your mind. *Try to **think** of the answer.*
2 If you **think** something, you believe it. *My brother **thinks** that hats are in fashion.*

# thirsty

**thirstier thirstiest**
When you are **thirsty**, you want to drink something.

# thorn

**thorns**
A **thorn** is a sharp point on the stem of a flower or a bush.

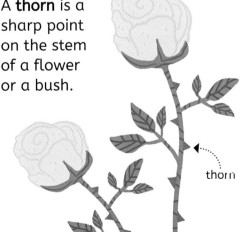

thorn

# thought

**thoughts**
A **thought** is something that you think. *Megan's mind was full of happy **thoughts**.*

# thought

**Thought** comes from the word **think**. *We tried to think of things to do. We **thought** very hard.*

# thread

**threads**
A **thread** is a long, thin length of cotton or wool. Thread is used for making cloth or for sewing.

# thread

**threads threading threaded**
When you **thread** a needle, you pass a thread through the hole in its end.

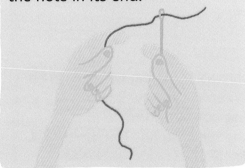

# threw

**Threw** comes from the word **throw**. *Throw the ball to me. Last time you **threw** it to Sarah.*

t

**219**

## throat

**throats**
1 Your **throat** is the front part of your neck.
2 Your **throat** is also the part inside your body that you use to swallow.

## throne

**thrones**
A **throne** is a special chair for a king or a queen.

*The queen sat on her golden* **throne**.

## through

When something goes **through**, it goes in one side and out the other. *We wandered* **through** *the woods.*

## throw

**throws throwing threw thrown**
When you **throw** something, you use your hand to send it through the air. *Tilly has* **thrown** *a stick for Fido.*

## thumb

**thumbs**
Your **thumb** is the short, thick finger on the side of each hand.

## thunder

**Thunder** is a loud, low sound that you sometimes hear when there is a storm.

## tick

**ticks**
1 A **tick** is a sign that shows that something is correct.
2 A **tick** is also the sound that a clock or a watch makes.

## ticket

**tickets**
A **ticket** is a small piece of paper or card that shows that you have paid for something. *A bus* **ticket**.

## tickle

**tickles tickling tickled**
If you **tickle** someone, you keep touching them with your fingers to make them laugh.

## tidy

**tidier tidiest**
A **tidy** room is neat, with everything in its proper place.

## tie

**ties**
1 A **tie** is a long strip of material that you wear knotted round your neck.
2 If a game is a **tie**, it is a draw.

# tie

**ties tying tied**
Tie means to hold things together by putting string, rope or ribbon around them, joined with a knot. *Jill **tied** a ribbon round the parcel. Dan **tied** the boat to the post.*

# tiger

**tigers**
A **tiger** is a very large wild cat. Tigers have orange fur with black stripes.

# tight

**tighter tightest**
1 Something that is **tight** is fastened firmly. *A **tight** knot.*
2 Clothes that are **tight** fit closely to your body. ***Tight** trousers.*
■ *opposite* **loose**

# tights

**Tights** cover your bottom, legs and feet. They are made out of stretchy material and fit very closely.

# time

**times**
1 **Time** is how long something takes to happen. Time is measured in seconds, minutes and hours. *It took a long **time** to walk home.*
2 The **time** is a particular moment, shown on a clock or a watch. *What **time** is it now?*

# timid

Someone who is **timid** is shy and easily frightened.

# tin

**tins**
1 **Tin** is a silver-coloured metal.
2 A **tin** is a small metal container. *A **tin** of beans.*

# tiny

**tinier tiniest**
Something that is **tiny** is very small. *A **tiny** insect.*

# tip

**tips**
1 The **tip** of something is the end of it. *The **tip** of a pen.*
2 A **tip** is also somewhere that you take your rubbish.

# tip

**tips tipping tipped**
When you **tip** something, you turn it over. *Henry **tipped** a bucket of water over Harriet's head.*

## tiptoe

**tiptoes tiptoeing tiptoed**
When you **tiptoe**, you walk very quietly without putting your heels down. *Stephen tiptoed across the hall.*

## tired

When you are **tired**, you want to rest or sleep.

## tissue

**tissues**
A **tissue** is a piece of soft, thin paper that you use to wipe your nose.

## title

**titles**
A **title** is the name by which something is known, such as a book, film or television programme.

## toad

**toads**
A **toad** is a small creature similar to a frog. Toads have rough, dry skin and live on land.

## toadstool

**toadstools**
A **toadstool** is a poisonous plant-like thing with a rounded top on a stalk.

## toast

**Toast** is bread that has been heated until it turns brown.

## today

**Today** is the day that is happening now. *I'm going to a birthday party **today**.*

## toddler

**toddlers**
A **toddler** is a young child who has just begun to walk.

## toe

**toes**
Your **toes** are the parts at the ends of your feet. You have five toes on each foot.

## toffee

**toffees**
A **toffee** is a chewy sweet that is made from butter and sugar.

## together

If people do something **together**, they do it with each other. *Zara and Luke played a game **together**.*

# toilet

**toilets**
A **toilet** is a bowl with a seat. When you go to the toilet, you get rid of waste food and liquid from your body and they are washed away with water.

# told

**Told** comes from the word **tell**. *Can you tell Skye to come inside? I've already **told** her twice.*

# tomato

**tomatoes**
A **tomato** is a soft, juicy fruit with a red skin. You use tomatoes to make salads.

# tomorrow

**Tomorrow** is the day after today. *We're going to the beach **tomorrow**.*

# tongue

**tongues**
▲ say *tung*
Your **tongue** is the long, soft part inside your mouth. You use your tongue to taste, eat and talk.

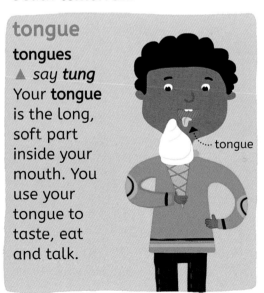

····· tongue

# tongue-twister

**tongue-twisters**
A **tongue-twister** is a sentence that is very hard to say quickly.

*The big black bug bit the big black bear, but the big black bear bit the big black bug back!*

# tonight

**Tonight** is the evening or night of this day. *We're staying in **tonight**.*

# too

1 **Too** means also.
*Is Ed here, **too**?*
2 **Too** also means more than enough. *That's **too** sweet for me.*

# took

**Took** comes from the word **take**. *Mum said we could take a biscuit. Liam **took** four!*

# tool

**tools**
A **tool** is something that you use to do a job.

# tooth

**teeth**
1 A **tooth** is one of the hard, white things inside your mouth. You use your teeth to bite and chew food.
2 A **tooth** is also one of a row of thin parts on a comb, a saw, a zip or a rake.

A B C D E F G H I J K L M N O P Q R S T U V W X Y Z

## toothbrush
**toothbrushes**
A **toothbrush** is a small brush with a long handle. You use a toothbrush to clean your teeth.

## toothpaste
**Toothpaste** is a thick paste that you use to clean your teeth.

## top
**tops**
1 The **top** is the highest point of something. *Carlos climbed to the **top** of the mountain.*
■ opposite **bottom**
2 The **top** of an object is also a kind of lid that fits over its end.
3 A **top** is also an item of clothing that covers the top part of your body.

## topic
**topics**
A **topic** is the name of something that you study. Children work on topics at school. *This term, our **topic** is weather.*

## torch
**torches**
A **torch** is a small lamp that you can carry around with you. Torches run on batteries.

## tore
**Tore** comes from the word **tear**. *Patrick must try not to tear his trousers. He **tore** his last pair when he went exploring.*

## tortoise
**tortoises**
A **tortoise** is an animal with thick, scaly skin and a shell on its back. Tortoises move very slowly.

## toss
**tosses tossing tossed**
If you **toss** something, you throw it into the air. *Aimee **tossed** the pancake and caught it in the pan.*

## total
**totals**
The **total** of a sum is its answer or its result. *Four is the **total** of two plus two.*

## touch
**touches touching touched**
If you **touch** something, you put part of your body against it.

## touch screen

**touch screens**
A **touch screen** is a screen on a computer or smartphone that you control by touching it instead of pressing buttons.

## tough

**tougher toughest**
▲ *rhymes with* **stuff**
**1** Something that is **tough** is hard to break or damage. *You'll need **tough** boots for this climb.*
**2** Someone who is **tough** is strong and is not afraid of getting hurt.

## tow

**tows towing towed**
When one vehicle **tows** another, it pulls it along. *The truck **towed** our car away.*

## towards

**Towards** means in the direction of something. *Abigail ran **towards** the castle.*

## towel

**towels**
A **towel** is a thick, soft piece of cloth that you use to dry your body.

## tower

**towers**
A **tower** is a tall, narrow building or part of a building.

## town

**towns**
A **town** is a place where many people live and work. Towns have houses, offices, schools and shops. Towns are smaller than cities.

## toy

**toys**
A **toy** is something that you play with.

## trace

**traces tracing traced**
When you **trace** a picture, you put a thin piece of paper over it and draw over its outline.

## track

**tracks**
**1** A **track** is a path.
**2** **Tracks** are marks left by the feet of a person or an animal. *We followed the fox's **tracks** into the wood.*

## tractor

**tractors**
A **tractor** is a strong vehicle with very large back wheels. Tractors are used on farms to pull machinery or heavy loads.

225

## traffic

**Traffic** is the name for all the vehicles travelling on the roads at the same time. *There's a lot of traffic in the centre of town.*

## traffic lights

**Traffic lights** are a set of lights that show traffic when to stop and go. Traffic lights are red, yellow and green.

## train

**trains**
A **train** is a vehicle that travels along a railway track.

## trainer

**trainers**
**Trainers** are soft shoes with rubber bottoms. People often wear them to play sports.

## tram

**trams**
A **tram** is a kind of bus that travels on rails in the road.

## trampoline

**trampolines**
A **trampoline** is a large piece of strong material attached to a frame with springs. You jump up and down on a trampoline.

## transparent

If something is **transparent**, it is clear and you can see through it. Glass and water are transparent.

## transport

**Transport** is the name for all the kinds of vehicles that take people or things from one place to another. *What kind of transport do you use to travel to school?*

## trap

**traps trapping trapped**
If you **trap** something, you catch it and stop it from escaping.

## travel

**travels travelling travelled**
When you **travel**, you go from one place to another. *We travel to school by car.*

## tray

**trays**
A **tray** is a flat piece of wood, metal or plastic that you use to carry food and drink.

## tread

**treads treading trod trodden**
When you **tread**, you put your foot down on something.
*Don't **tread** on the flowers!*

## treasure

**Treasure** is a name for valuable things, such as gold and jewels. *The pirates buried a chest full of **treasure**.*

## treat

**treats**
A **treat** is a special present or a trip to somewhere nice. *Mum took us to the cinema as a **treat**.*

## treat

**treats treating treated**
1 The way you **treat** someone is the way you behave towards them. *Darvesh **treats** his little sister very well.*
2 When doctors **treat** people who are ill, they try to make them better.

## tree

**trees**
A **tree** is a very large plant with leaves, branches and a trunk.

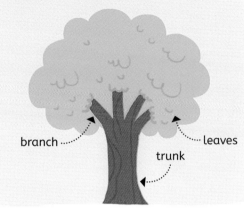

branch ···· leaves
trunk

## triangle

**triangles**
1 A **triangle** is a shape with three straight sides.
2 A **triangle** is also a musical instrument that is made of metal and shaped like a triangle. You play a triangle by hitting it with a metal stick.

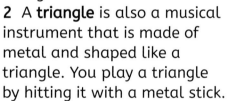

## trick

**tricks**
1 If you do a **trick**, you do something clever and surprising.
2 If you **play a trick** on someone, you make them believe something that is not true.

## tricycle

**tricycles**
A **tricycle** is like a bicycle, but has two wheels at the back and one at the front.

t

**227**

## tried

**Tried** comes from the word **try**. *Lewis will try to move the box. He has **tried** twice already.*

## trip

**trips**
When you go on a **trip**, you travel to a place and then come back. *We went on a **trip** to the zoo.*

## trip

**trips tripping tripped**
If you **trip**, you hit your foot on something and fall or nearly fall. *Natasha **tripped** over the toys on the floor.*

## troll

**trolls**
1 In stories, a **troll** is a big, ugly, stupid monster.
2 A **troll** is someone who posts nasty comments on the internet to upset people or start arguments.

## trolley

**trolleys**
A **trolley** is a large basket on wheels. *A supermarket **trolley**.*

## trophy

**trophies**
A **trophy** is a prize that you are given to show that you did well at something. *This year, our team won the swimming **trophy**.*

## trouble

1 **Trouble** is something that is difficult or dangerous. *The farmer had **trouble** rescuing his sheep.*
2 If you are **in trouble**, you have done something wrong and someone is angry with you.

## trousers

**trousers**
**Trousers** are clothes that cover your legs.

## truck

**trucks**
A **truck** is a large vehicle that carries things from place to place.

## true

1 If something is **true**, it is correct or right.
■ *opposite* **false**
2 If a story is **true**, it really happened.

## trumpet

**trumpets**
A **trumpet** is a musical instrument made of metal. You play a trumpet by blowing into it.

## trunk

**trunks**
1 A **trunk** is the thick stem of a tree.
2 An elephant's **trunk** is its long nose. Elephants use their trunks to suck up water and to pick things up.

trunk

3 A **trunk** is also a large, strong box that you keep things in.

## trust

**trusts trusting trusted**
If you **trust** someone, you think that they are honest and will keep their promises.

## truth

If you tell the **truth**, what you say is true.

## try

**tries trying tried**
1 When you **try** to do something, you do it as well as you can. *Mel **tried** to climb the wall.*
2 If you **try** something, you test it to see what it is like. *Daisy **tried** the rice to see if it was cooked.*

## T-shirt

**T-shirts**
A **T-shirt** is a piece of clothing that you wear on the top part of your body. T-shirts usually have short sleeves and round necks with no collar.

## tube

**tubes**
1 A **tube** is something that is long, round and hollow. *A **tube** of sweets.*
2 A **tube** is also a container for soft mixtures, such as toothpaste. You squeeze the tube to get the mixture out.

## tug

**tugs tugging tugged**
If you **tug** something, you pull it hard.

# tune

**tunes**
A **tune** is a group of musical notes arranged in a special order. Tunes are usually pleasant to listen to.

# tunnel

**tunnels**
A **tunnel** is a long passage under the ground.

# turban

**turbans**
A **turban** is a long piece of cloth that some men and boys wear wrapped round their heads.

# turkey

**turkeys**
1 A **turkey** is a large bird that is kept on a farm.
2 **Turkey** is also a kind of meat that comes from turkeys.

# turn

**turns**
If it is your **turn** to do something, it is your time to do it. *It's Tom's **turn** to use the computer.*

# turn

**turns turning turned**
1 When you **turn**, you move in a different direction. *The car **turned** left.*
2 If something **turns**, it moves around in a circle.
3 If you **turn** a machine **on** or **off**, you make it start or stop.
4 If a thing **turns into** something else, it changes into it. *The frog **turned into** a handsome prince.*

# turtle

**turtles**
A **turtle** is an animal with thick, scaly skin and a shell on its back. Turtles live in water.

# tusk

**tusks**
An elephant's **tusks** are its two long, pointed teeth on either side of its trunk.

# twice

If something happens **twice**, it happens two times.

# twig

**twigs**
A **twig** is a small, thin branch of a tree or a bush.

## twin

**twins**
**Twins** are two children who have the same parents and were born on the same day. Twins often look alike.

## twist

**twists twisting twisted**
When you **twist** something, you turn part of it while holding the rest of it still.

## tying

**Tying** comes from the word **tie**. *Kim is learning to tie knots. She has been tying knots for hours.*

## type

**types**
Things of the same **type** belong to the same group. *Poppies are a type of flower.*

## type

**types typing typed**
When you **type**, you write something using a keyboard.

## tyre

**tyres**
A **tyre** is a circle of strong rubber that fits round a wheel. Tyres are usually full of air.

# Uu

## ugly

**uglier ugliest**
Something that is **ugly** is not nice to look at. *An ugly building. An ugly monster.*

## umbrella

**umbrellas**
You hold an **umbrella** over your head to keep the rain off. An umbrella is made of a piece of cloth or plastic stretched over a frame.

Many words are given the opposite meaning by adding **un** to the start. For example: able – **un**able; do – **un**do.

## unable

If you are **unable** to do something, you cannot do it. *Leo is unable to come tonight.*

## uncle

**uncles**
Your **uncle** is the brother of your mum or dad.

## uncomfortable

If something is **uncomfortable**, it does not feel good. *Uncomfortable shoes. An uncomfortable chair.*

## under

**1** If something is **under** another thing, it is lower than it, or underneath it. *Amy checked for monsters under her bed.*
**2** **Under** also means less than. *Josh ran the race in under three minutes.*
■ opposite **over**

## underline

**underlines underlining underlined**
If you **underline** something, you draw a line under it.

## underneath

If one thing is **underneath** another thing, it is in the space under it. *My toys are underneath my bed.*

## understand

**understands understanding understood**
If you **understand** something, you know what it means or how it works.

## underwear

**Underwear** is the name for the clothes that you wear under your other clothes. Vests and pants are kinds of underwear.

## undress

**undresses undressing undressed**
When you **undress**, you take off your clothes.

## unemployed

Someone who is **unemployed** does not have a job.

## unhappy

**unhappier unhappiest**
If you are **unhappy**, you are sad or upset.

## uniform

**uniforms**
A **uniform** is a special set of clothes worn by all the members of a group. *A school uniform.*

## unit

**units**
A **unit** is a fixed amount of something. Units are used for counting or for measuring things. *A minute is a unit of time.*
*A pound is a unit of money.*

## universe

The **universe** is everything that is in space. The Earth, Sun, Moon and stars are all parts of the universe.

# unkind

**unkinder unkindest**
An **unkind** person is unpleasant and not helpful.

# unlucky

**unluckier unluckiest**
If you are **unlucky**, bad things happen to you that are not your fault.

# unpleasant

If something is **unpleasant**, it is horrible or nasty. *An **unpleasant** smell.*

# untidy

**untidier untidiest**
If something is **untidy**, it is messy and not neat.

# until

**Until** means up to the time that something happens.

*I am looking after Tom's fish **until** he comes back from holiday.*

# unusual

If something is **unusual**, it is not normal, or is not what you would expect. *Jasmine was wearing an **unusual** hat. It's **unusual** for it to be so hot in February.*

# up

When something moves **up**, it goes from a lower place to a higher place. *We pushed our bikes **up** the hill.*
■ opposite **down**

# upon

**Upon** means on top of. *The cat sat **upon** the step.*

# upright

**Upright** means standing up straight.

# upset

If you are **upset**, you are unhappy or angry. *Rosie was very **upset** when her cat died.*

# upside down

**1** If you turn something **upside down**, you put its top where its bottom should be. *Leon turned the bucket **upside down** to make a seat.*
**2** If you hang **upside down**, your head is below your feet.

*Anna loves hanging **upside down**.*

233

## urgent

If something is **urgent**, you need to do something about it quickly.

## use

**uses using used**
▲ *rhymes with* **choose**
When you **use** something, you do a job with it. *Jayden used scissors to cut the card.*

## useful

If something is **useful**, it helps you to do something.

## usual

If something is **usual**, it is what you would expect. *I'll be home at the usual time.*

## usually

If something is **usually** happens, it happens most of the time.

## vacuum cleaner

**vacuum cleaners**
A **vacuum cleaner** is a machine that you use to clean the floor. Vacuum cleaners suck up dirt and dust.

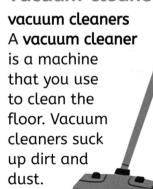

## valley

**valleys**
A **valley** is an area of low ground between mountains or hills. Rivers often run through valleys.

## valuable

**1** Something that is **valuable** is worth a lot of money. *Mum has a valuable ring.*
**2** **Valuable** also means important. *Valuable information.*

## van

**vans**
A **van** is a vehicle that is used for carrying things.

## vanish

**vanishes vanishing vanished**
If something **vanishes**, it disappears suddenly. *The rabbit vanished from the magician's hat.*

## vase

**vases**
▲ *say* **varz**
A **vase** is a kind of jar. You can put flowers in a vase or you can use it as an ornament.

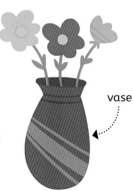

vase

# vegetable
**vegetables**
A **vegetable** is a plant that you can eat. Potatoes, carrots and peas are all vegetables.

# vegetarian
**vegetarians**
A **vegetarian** is someone who does not eat meat or fish.

# vehicle
**vehicles**
▲ *say vee-ickle*
A **vehicle** is a machine that carries people or things from one place to another. Bicycles, cars and trains are all vehicles.

# verse
**verses**
A **verse** is a part of a poem or a song. *We sang all five verses of the song.*

# very
**Very** means a lot. *I am very excited about going on holiday.*

# vest
**vests**
A **vest** is a piece of underwear that you wear on the top part of your body.

# vet
**vets**
A **vet** is someone who helps sick animals to get better.

# video
**videos**
When you watch a **video**, you see moving pictures with sound. People often watch videos on the internet.

# view
**views**
1 A **view** is what you can see from a particular place. *I have a view of the beach from my window.*
2 A **view** is what you think about something. *What is your view of this book?*

# village
**villages**
A **village** is a small group of houses and other buildings in the country.

# vinegar
**Vinegar** is a liquid that you use to add flavour to food. Vinegar tastes sour.

235

A B C D E F G H I J K L M N O P Q R S T U V W X Y Z

## violent

If something is **violent**, it is very strong and damages things. *A **violent** storm.*

## violin

**violins**
A **violin** is a musical instrument with strings. You hold a violin under your chin and move a bow across its strings.

violin
bow

## visit

**visits visiting visited**
If you **visit** someone, you go to see them. *I **visited** my granny yesterday afternoon.*

## visitor

**visitors**
A **visitor** is someone who comes to your house to see you or to stay with you.

## vital

If something is **vital**, it is very important. ***Vital** information.*

## voice

**voices**
Your **voice** is the sound that you make when you talk or sing. *Ruth has a high **voice**.*

## volcano

**volcanoes** or **volcanos**
A **volcano** is a mountain with a hole in the top. Sometimes hot, liquid rock and gas burst out of a volcano.

## volume

**volumes**
1 The **volume** of a sound is how loud it is.
2 The **volume** of an object is how much space it takes up.
3 A **volume** is one of a set of books. *This set of encyclopedias has six **volumes**.*

## volunteer

**volunteers**
A **volunteer** is someone who offers to do something.

## vote

**votes voting voted**
1 When you **vote** for something, you show that you agree with it.
2 When you **vote** for a person, you show that you support them. *My dad says **voting** is important.*

## vowel

**vowels**
A **vowel** is one of the letters a, e, i, o, u.

## voyage

**voyages**
A **voyage** is a long journey, especially one by sea.

## wade

**wades wading waded**
When you **wade**, you walk through quite deep water.

## wagon

**wagons**
A **wagon** was a vehicle used in the past for carrying loads. Wagons had four wheels and were often pulled by horses.

## waist

**waists**
Your **waist** is the narrow, middle part of your body, below your chest.

## waistcoat

**waistcoats**
A **waistcoat** is a short jacket with no sleeves.

## wait

**waits waiting waited**
When you **wait**, you stay in a place until something happens. *James **waited** for Charlotte to arrive at the station.*

## waiter

**waiters**
A **waiter** is a man who serves people with food or drink in a restaurant or a café.

## waitress

**waitresses**
A **waitress** is a woman who serves people with food or drink in a restaurant or a café.

## wake

**wakes waking woke woken**
When you **wake up**, you stop sleeping. *Josiah **woke up** early.*

## walk

**walks walking walked**
When you **walk**, you move along by putting one foot in front of the other. *Katie always **walks** to school.*

Some other words for **walk** are **stride**, **stroll**, **march** and **hike**.

a b c d e f g h i j k l m n o p q r s t u v w x y z

## wallpaper

**wallpapers**
**Wallpaper** is paper that people stick to walls. Wallpaper sometimes has patterns on it.

## wander

**wanders wandering wandered**
If you **wander**, you walk around without deciding where to go. *Jonathan **wandered** around the shops.*

## want

**wants wanting wanted**
If you **want** something, you would like it. *Ella **wanted** some chocolate.*

## war

**wars**
In a **war**, armies fight each other over a long period of time.

## wardrobe

**wardrobes**
A **wardrobe** is a cupboard that you keep your clothes in. *Ed hung his jacket in the **wardrobe**.*

## warm

**warmer warmest**
Something that is **warm** is quite hot. *A **warm** day.*

## warn

**warns warning warned**
If you **warn** someone, you tell them about something dangerous or bad that may happen. *Phoebe **warned** us that the path was very steep.*

## was

**Was** comes from the word **be**. *I will be at the swimming pool later. I **was** there yesterday, too.*

## wash

**washes washing washed**
When you **wash** something, you clean it with soap and water.

*Millie and Dan **washed** their dad's car.*

## washing machine

**washing machines**
A **washing machine** is a machine that washes clothes.

## wasn't

**Wasn't** is a short way of saying **was not**. *Becky **wasn't** interested in playing the game.*

## wasp

**wasps**
A **wasp** is an insect with black and yellow stripes. Wasps can sting.

## waste

**wastes wasting wasted**
If you **waste** something, you use more of it than you need to, or you use it for something that isn't important. *Don't waste your money on sweets.*

## watch

**watches**
A **watch** is a small clock that you wear on your wrist.

## watch

**watches watching watched**
1 If you **watch** something, you look at it to see what happens.
2 You tell someone to **watch out** when you warn them to be careful. *Watch out for that step!*

## water

**Water** is the clear liquid in rivers, seas and rain. Water also comes out of taps. People, animals and plants need water to live.

## waterfall

**waterfalls**
A **waterfall** is a place where water from a river falls down over rocks.

## wave

**waves**
A **wave** is the water that rises and falls on the surface of the sea. *The children jumped over the waves.*

## wave

**waves waving waved**
When you **wave**, you move your hand from side to side. You wave to say hello or goodbye.

## wax

**Wax** is a soft material that melts when it is heated. Wax is used to make candles and crayons.

## way

**ways**
1 The **way** you do something is how you do it. *Is this the right way to spell your name?*
2 A **way** is how you get from one place to another.
*Tell me the way home.*

a b c d e f g h i j k l m n o p q r s t u v w x y z

A B C D E F G H I J K L M N O P Q R S T U V W X Y Z

## weak

**weaker weakest**
1 A **weak** person is not strong and does not have much energy.
2 Something that is **weak** breaks easily. *This chair has weak legs.*

## weapon

**weapons**
A **weapon** is a tool for fighting. Guns and swords are weapons.

## wear

**wears wearing wore worn**
1 When you **wear** clothes, they cover your body. *Max wore his green jacket.*
2 If something **wears out**, it becomes less useful because it has been used so much. *Grace's shoes are wearing out.*

## weather

The **weather** is what it is like outside, such as hot or cold, rainy or sunny.

## web

**webs**
1 A **web** is a very thin net that a spider makes to catch insects.
2 **The web** is also short for the world wide web, a huge collection of web pages on the internet that are linked to each other.

## web page

**web pages**
A **web page** is an electronic page on the internet.

## website

**websites**
A **website** is a group of web pages that are linked to each other.

## we'd

1 **We'd** is a short way of saying **we had**. *We'd just reached the forest when it started to rain.*
2 **We'd** is also a short way of saying **we would**. *We'd love to come to your party.*

## wedding

**weddings**
When two people have a **wedding**, they get married.

## week

**weeks**
A **week** is a period of seven days. There are fifty-two weeks in a year.

## weekend

**weekends**
The **weekend** is Saturday and Sunday. *We often go cycling at the weekend.*

## weigh

**weighs weighing weighed**
When you **weigh** something, you find out how heavy it is. *Shauna weighed the sugar on the scales.*

## weight

**weights**
Your **weight** is how heavy you are. *Do you know your weight?*

## welcome

**welcomes welcoming welcomed**
If you **welcome** someone, you are friendly to them when they arrive. *We rushed to welcome our grandparents.*

## we'll

**We'll** is a short way of saying **we will**. *We'll come and see you at the weekend.*

## well

**wells**
A **well** is a deep hole in the ground. People dig wells to reach water, oil or gas.

## well

**better best**
1 If you do something **well**, you are good at it. *Edward plays the violin well.*
2 If you are **well**, you are healthy or happy. *Bert is looking very well.*

## went

**Went** comes from the word **go**. *Carolyn likes to go to the beach. She went there last week with some friends.*

## we're

**We're** is a short way of saying **we are**. *We're going on holiday tomorrow.*

## were

**Were** comes from the word **be**. *The children tried to be quiet. They were silent for almost two minutes.*

a b c d e f g h i j k l m n o p q r s t u v w x y z

## weren't

**Weren't** is a short way of saying **were not**. *We **weren't** allowed to stay up late.*

## west

**West** is a direction. The Sun goes down in the west.
■ *opposite* **east**

## wet

**wetter wettest**
If something is **wet**, it has liquid on it. *A **wet** towel.*
■ *opposite* **dry**

## we've

**We've** is a short way of saying **we have**. *We've been to the park.*

## whale

**whales**
A **whale** is a very big animal that lives in the sea. A whale breathes through a hole in the top of its head.

blue whale

## what

You use the word **what** to find out more about something. *What is your name?*

## what's

1 **What's** is a short way of saying **what is**. *What's the time?*
2 **What's** is also a short way of saying **what has**. *What's happened to your hair?*

## wheat

**Wheat** is a plant that is grown on farms. Wheat is used to make flour.

## wheel

**wheels**
A **wheel** is round and can turn in a circle. Cars, bicycles and roller skates use wheels to move along.

## wheelbarrow

**wheelbarrows**
You use a **wheelbarrow** to carry things in a garden. A wheelbarrow has a wheel at the front and handles so that you can push it along.

## wheelchair

**wheelchairs**
A **wheelchair** is a chair on wheels. People who cannot walk use a wheelchair to get from place to place.

## when

You use the word **when** to talk or ask about the time of something. **When** *did you last see Marcus?*

## where

You use the word **where** to talk or ask about a place. **Where** *are you?*

## where's

1 **Where's** is a short way of saying **where is**. **Where's** *my football?*
2 **Where's** is also a short way of saying **where has**. **Where's** *Jacob gone?*

## which

You use the word **which** to ask about one of a number of things. **Which** *shirt shall I wear?*

## while

1 **While** means in the time that something is happening. *Sam fed my cat **while** I was away.*
2 **While** also means a period of time. *It's a long **while** since we first met.*

## whiskers

**Whiskers** are the long hairs that grow near the nose of some animals, such as mice, cats and rabbits. *My pet mouse has very long **whiskers**.*

## whisper

**whispers whispering whispered**
When you **whisper**, you talk very quietly.

## whistle

**whistles**
A **whistle** is a small tube that makes a high, loud sound when you blow into it.

## whistle

**whistles whistling whistled**
When you **whistle**, you make a sound or a tune by blowing through your lips.

## white

**White** is a colour.
Snow is white.

## whiteboard

**whiteboards**
A **whiteboard** is a board that
teachers write on, with special
pens that can be wiped off.

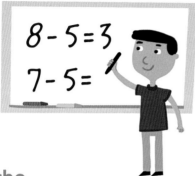

$$8 - 5 = 3$$
$$7 - 5 =$$

## who

▲ Say **hoo**
You use the word **who** to talk
or ask about someone.
**Who** won the race?

## who'd

1 **Who'd** is a short way of
saying **who had**. *Rosa was the
only one* **who'd** *seen the film.*
2 **Who'd** is also a short way
of saying **who would**.
**Who'd** *like to come?*

## whole

**Whole** means all of something.
*George has eaten a* **whole**
*packet of biscuits.*

## who'll

**Who'll** is a short way of saying
**who will**. **Who'll** *come with me?*

## who's

▲ Say **hooze**
1 **Who's** is a short way of
saying **who is**. **Who's**
*going to the fair?*
2 **Who's** is also a short way
of saying **who has**. **Who's** *been
eating my porridge?*

## whose

▲ Say **hooze**
You use **whose** to talk or ask
about who or what things
belong to. **Whose** *gloves
are these?*

## why

You use the word **why** to talk
or ask about the reason for
something. **Why** *are you upset?*

## wicked

Someone who
is **wicked** is very
bad. *The* **wicked**
*witch waved
her wand.*

## wide

**wider widest**
If something is **wide**, it measures
a lot from one side to the other.
*A* **wide** *table.*
■ opposite **narrow**

## width

**widths**
The **width** of something is how far it is from one side to the other.

## wife

**wives**
Someone's **wife** is the woman they are married to.

## wig

**wigs**
A **wig** is false hair that fits on someone's head.

## wild

**wilder wildest**
**Wild** animals and plants are not looked after by people.
■ *opposite* **tame**

*A **wild** bird.*

## wildlife

**Wildlife** is a name for wild animals, insects and plants.

## will

**would**
If someone **will** do something, they are going to do it.
*Jake **will** tidy up later.*

## willing

If you are **willing** to do something, you don't mind doing it.

## win

**wins winning won**
If you **win** a race or a game, you come first.
■ *opposite* **lose**

## wind

▲ *rhymes with* **tinned**
**Wind** is air that moves quickly.
*The **wind** blew Hattie's hat off.*

## wind

**winds winding wound**
▲ *rhymes with* **kind**
**1** If you **wind** something **around** another thing, you put it around it several times. *Rollo **wound** his scarf **around** his neck.*
**2** When you **wind up** a clock or a toy, you turn its key to make it work.
**3** If a road or a river **winds**, it has lots of bends and turns.

## windmill

**windmills**
A **windmill** is a tall building with large sails. When the wind turns the sails, a machine inside the windmill turns grain into flour.

a b c d e f g h i j k l m n o p q r s t u v w x y z

A B C D E F G H I J K L M N O P Q R S T U V W X Y Z

## window
**windows**
A **window** is a space in a wall or a vehicle that lets in light and air. Windows are usually filled with glass.

## wing
**wings**
**Wings** make things able to fly. Birds, bats, insects and planes all have wings.

## wink
**winks winking winked**
When you **wink**, you close and open one eye very quickly. You wink to show that something is a joke or a secret.

## winner
**winners**
The **winner** of a race or a game is the person who comes in first place.

## winter
**Winter** is one of the four seasons. It comes between autumn and spring. Winter is the coldest season.

## wipe
**wipes wiping wiped**
When you **wipe** something, you rub it with a cloth to make it clean.

## wire
**wires**
A **wire** is a long, thin piece of metal that bends easily. Wires can be used to carry electricity or to fasten things.

## wise
**wiser wisest**
**Wise** people know the right thing to say and do.

## wish
**wishes wishing wished**
If you **wish** that something would happen, you want it to happen very much.

## witch
**witches**
A **witch** is a woman with magic powers who you read about in stories.

## with
1 If you do something **with** someone, you both do it together.
2 You also use **with** to show that someone has something. *I know a boy **with** green eyes.*
3 The word **with** also shows what you use to do something. *Natasha loves eating chicken **with** her fingers.*

## without

If you are **without** something, you do not have it. *Alex came to school **without** his packed lunch.*

## wizard

**wizards**
A **wizard** is a man with magic powers who you read about in stories.

## wobble

**wobbles wobbling wobbled**
If something **wobbles**, it moves from side to side. *The jelly **wobbled** on the plate.*

## woke

**Woke** comes from the word **wake**. *Anna usually wakes up early, but today she **woke** up late.*

## wolf

**wolves**
A **wolf** is a wild animal that looks like a large dog. Wolves have thick coats. They live in forests and hunt in groups.

## woman

**women**
A **woman** is an adult, female human being.

## won

**Won** comes from the word **win**. *Our team hopes to win today. We have **won** our last five games.*

## wonder

**wonders wondering wondered**
If you **wonder** what to do, you are not sure what you should do. *Jessie **wondered** which path she should take.*

## won't

**Won't** is a short way of saying **will not**. *Meg **won't** let her brother come into her room.*

## wood

**woods**
1 **Wood** comes from the trunks and branches of trees. It is used in building and to make things such as furniture.
2 A **wood** is a place where lots of trees grow close together. Woods are smaller than forests.

## wooden

Something that is **wooden** is made from wood. *A **wooden** spoon.*

## wool

**Wool** is the hair that grows on sheep. Wool is made into thread and used for knitting or making cloth.

## word

**words**
A **word** is a group of sounds or letters that means something. You use words when you speak or write.

## wore

**Wore** comes from the word **wear**. *Kim didn't know what to wear. In the end, she wore her jeans.*

## work

**works working worked**
1 When people **work**, they do a job. *My mum works in a hospital.*
2 If you **work**, you use your energy to do something. *Zack is working hard at maths.*
3 If something **works**, it does what it is meant to do. *Our radio is working again.*

## world

The **world** is the Earth, and everything that lives on it.

## worm

**worms**
A **worm** is a small animal with a long, thin body and no legs. Worms live in the ground.

## worn

**Worn** comes from the word **wear**. *Emily likes to wear big hats. She has worn a hat every day this week.*

## worry

**worries worrying worried**
If you **worry**, you keep thinking about bad things that might happen.

## worse

**Worse** means less good. *Your handwriting is worse than mine.*
■ *opposite* **better**

## worst

**Worst** means worse than anything else. *This is the worst film I have ever seen.*
■ *opposite* **best**

## worth

If something is **worth** an amount of money, it could be sold for that amount. *This painting is worth a lot of money.*

## would

**Would** comes from the word **will**. *I will come to see you this week. I would have come last week, but I was busy.*

## wouldn't

**Wouldn't** is a short way of saying **would not**. *Amy wouldn't lend her brother any money.*

## wound

**wounds**
▲ *rhymes with* **spooned**
A **wound** is a cut in your skin. Wounds are usually quite deep.

## wound

▲ *rhymes with* **sound**
**Wound** comes from the word **wind**. *Jo started to wind the wool. She wound it around her hand.*

## wrap

**wraps wrapping wrapped**
When you **wrap** an object, you cover it with something, such as paper or cloth. *Ethan wrapped Kieran's present in red paper.*

## wrapper

**wrappers**
A **wrapper** is a piece of paper or plastic that covers something. *A sweet wrapper.*

## wreck

**wrecks wrecking wrecked**
If you **wreck** something, you completely destroy it. *My uncle was in a car accident. He's okay, but his car was wrecked.*

## wrestle

**wrestles wrestling wrestled**
When people **wrestle**, they fight and try to throw each other to the ground.

## wrinkle

**wrinkles**
A **wrinkle** is a line on someone's skin. *The old man's face was covered with wrinkles.*

## wrist

**wrists**
Your **wrist** is the joint between your arm and your hand.

## write

**writes writing wrote written**
1  When you **write**, you use a pen or pencil to put words or numbers on paper.
2  When you **write** a story, you make it up, then put it on paper or type it on a computer. *Amelia is writing a story about a dragon.*

## writing

**Writing** is anything that has been written.

## written

**Written** comes from the word **write**. *Polly writes to Ali regularly. She has **written** every week since she moved house.*

## wrong

1 Something that is **wrong** is not correct. *Some of my answers were **wrong**.*
2 If people do something **wrong**, they do something bad.
■ opposite **right**

## wrote

**Wrote** comes from the word **write**. *William likes to write poems. Last week, he **wrote** a brilliant poem about a tiger.*

## x-ray

**x-rays**
An **x-ray** is a kind of photograph that shows the inside of someone's body.

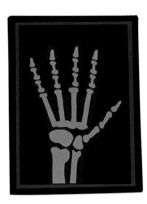

## xylophone

**xylophones**
▲ say **zy**-loh-fone
A **xylophone** is a musical instrument with a row of wooden bars. You play a xylophone by hitting the bars with small hammers.

## yacht

**yachts**
▲ say **yot**
A **yacht** is a boat with big sails. Most yachts also have engines.

## yawn

**yawns yawning yawned**
When you **yawn**, you open your mouth wide and breathe in deeply. You yawn because you are tired or bored.

## year

**years**
1 A **year** is the time from 1st January to 31st December.
2 A **year** is also any period of 12 months.

## yell

**yells yelling yelled**
If you **yell**, you shout or scream very loudly. *Felix **yelled** for help.*

## yellow

**Yellow** is a colour. Lemons and butter are yellow.

## yesterday

**Yesterday** means the day before today.

## yet

**Yet** means up to this time. *Jon hasn't called **yet**.*

## yogurt

**Yogurt** is a thick liquid food that is made from milk.

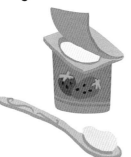

## yolk

**yolks**
▲ say **yoke**
The **yolk** is the yellow part in the middle of an egg.

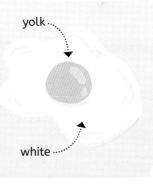

yolk

white

## you

**You** is a word that you use when you speak to someone else, or to a group of people. *How are **you** feeling?*

## you'd

1 **You'd** is a short way of saying **you had**. *You'd already left when I came round.*
2 **You'd** is also a short way of saying **you would**. *You'd have loved the museum.*

## you'll

**You'll** is a short way of saying **you will**. *You'll get cold if you don't wear a coat.*

## young

**younger youngest**
▲ say **yung**
Someone who is **young** has lived for only a short time.
■ opposite **old**

## your

**Your** means belonging to you. *Please would you hang **your** coats in the hall.*

## you're

**You're** is a short way of saying **you are**. *You're late again!*

## yours

If something belongs to **you**, then it is **yours**. *I've lost my ruler. Can I borrow **yours**?*

## yourself

**Yourself** means you and nobody else. *Help **yourself** to some food.*

a b c d e f g h i j k l m n o p q r s t u v w x y z

## you've

**You've** is a short way of saying **you have**. *You've eaten far too much cake!*

## yo-yo

**yo-yos**
A **yo-yo** is a toy that rolls up and down on a string that you loop round your finger.

# Zz

## zebra

**zebras**
A **zebra** is an animal with black and white stripes on its body. Zebras look like horses and live in herds, in Africa.

## zigzag

**zigzags**
A **zigzag** is a line that goes up and down.

## zip

**zips**
**Zips** are sewn into clothes and bags and are used to fasten them. A zip has two rows of metal or plastic teeth that fit together when you do it up.

## zoo

**zoos**
A **zoo** is a place where animals are kept for people to see.

252

## Numbers

| | |
|---|---|
| 0 | zero or nought |
| 1 | one |
| 2 | two |
| 3 | three |
| 4 | four |
| 5 | five |
| 6 | six |
| 7 | seven |
| 8 | eight |
| 9 | nine |
| 10 | ten |
| 11 | eleven |
| 12 | twelve |
| 13 | thirteen |
| 14 | fourteen |
| 15 | fifteen |
| 16 | sixteen |
| 17 | seventeen |
| 18 | eighteen |
| 19 | nineteen |
| 20 | twenty |
| 21 | twenty-one |
| 30 | thirty |
| 40 | forty |
| 50 | fifty |
| 60 | sixty |
| 70 | seventy |
| 80 | eighty |
| 90 | ninety |
| 100 | hundred |
| 1000 | thousand |

## Order

| | |
|---|---|
| 1st | first |
| 2nd | second |
| 3rd | third |
| 4th | fourth |
| 5th | fifth |
| 6th | sixth |
| 7th | seventh |
| 8th | eighth |
| 9th | ninth |
| 10th | tenth |
| 11th | eleventh |
| 12th | twelfth |
| 13th | thirteenth |
| 14th | fourteenth |
| 15th | fifteenth |
| 16th | sixteenth |
| 17th | seventeenth |
| 18th | eighteenth |
| 19th | nineteenth |
| 20th | twentieth |
| 21st | twenty-first |
| 30th | thirtieth |
| 40th | fortieth |
| 50th | fiftieth |
| 60th | sixtieth |
| 70th | seventieth |
| 80th | eightieth |
| 90th | ninetieth |
| 100th | hundredth |
| 1000th | thousandth |

## Days of the week

Monday
Tuesday
Wednesday
Thursday
Friday
Saturday
Sunday

## Months of the year

January
February
March
April
May
June
July
August
September
October
November
December

## Seasons

spring
summer
autumn
winter

## Colours of the rainbow

red

orange

yellow

green

blue

indigo

violet

## Measurements

### Length

1 millimetre (mm)
1 centimetre (cm) = 10mm
1 metre (m) = 100cm
1 kilometre (km) = 1,000m

### Volume

1 millilitre (ml)
1 centilitre (cl) = 10ml
1 litre (l) = 100cl
1 kilolitre (kl) = 1,000l

### Weight

1 milligram (mg)
1 gram (g) = 1,000mg
1 kilogram (kg) = 1,000g
1 tonne (t) = 1,000kg

### Temperature

°C = degrees Celsius
0°C = water freezes
37°C = body temperature
100°C = water boils

## The planets

Mercury      Jupiter
Venus        Saturn
Earth        Uranus
Mars         Neptune

## Directions

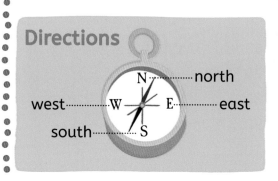

# Continents and oceans

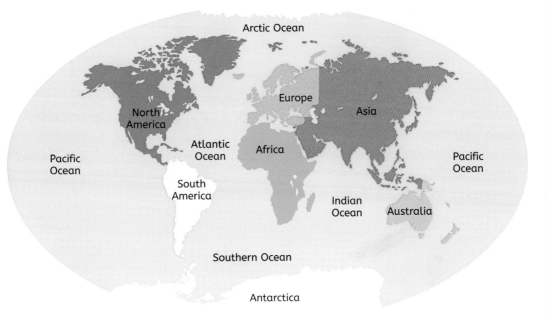

## Spelling quiz

For each question, choose the correct spelling: **a** or **b**. You can check your answers on page 256.

1. **a** seperate   **b** separate
2. **a** arguement   **b** argument
3. **a** forty   **b** fourty
4. **a** foriegn   **b** foreign
5. **a** calendar   **b** calender
6. **a** receive   **b** recieve
7. **a** until   **b** untill
8. **a** sensable   **b** sensible
9. **a** beginning   **b** begining
10. **a** allmost   **b** almost
11. **a** freind   **b** friend
12. **a** library   **b** libary

## Word hunt

Search this dictionary for the answers to these questions. Check them on page 256.

1. What does an **anchor** do?
2. What is the **capital** city of Japan?
3. What is **CD** short for?
4. What does **hibernate** mean?
5. What does a **microscope** do?
6. How many legs does an **octopus** have?
7. What do **pandas** eat?
8. What is **steel** mostly made of?
9. How long does the Earth take to go around the **Sun**?
10. How does a **whale** breathe?

# Answers

**Page 255** Spelling quiz

**1.** b **2.** b **3.** a **4.** b **5.** a **6.** a **7.** a **8.** b **9.** a **10.** b **11.** b **12.** a

**Page 255** Word hunt

**1.** It stops a ship from moving. **2.** Tokyo **3.** compact disc **4.** To sleep through the winter. **5.** It makes things look much bigger. **6.** eight **7.** bamboo **8.** iron **9.** a year **10.** Through a hole in the top of its head.

## Acknowledgements

Additional illustrations by Candice Whatmore and Lizzie Barber
Digital manipulation by Keith Furnival
Proofreading by Hannah Rowley and Simon Tudhope